Robert William Dale

Nine Lectures on Preaching

Delivered at Yale, New Haven, Connecticut

Robert William Dale

Nine Lectures on Preaching
Delivered at Yale, New Haven, Connecticut

ISBN/EAN: 9783337003227

Printed in Europe, USA, Canada, Australia, Japan

Cover: Foto ©Lupo / pixelio.de

More available books at **www.hansebooks.com**

NINE LECTURES

ON

PREACHING.

DELIVERED AT YALE, NEW HAVEN, CONNECTICUT.

BY

R. W. DALE,
Birmingham.

Immo vero audi quod dicis, quicumque dicis; et qui vis te audiri prior te audi.—*Augustine.*

PREFACE.

IF I rightly understand the objects for which the Lyman Beecher Lectureship was founded, the Lecturer is not expected to deliver a complete and systematic course on Homiletics. He discharges his duty if he offers to the students whom he has the honour of addressing those practical suggestions with regard to the work of the Christian Preacher which have been verified by his own experience and observation.

It is possible that the religious thought and life of America are in some respects so different from the religious thought and life of England, that very much of what I have written may be of no service to those who are being educated for the American ministry. But I was obliged to speak of the work of the Christian Preacher as I know it best. I have tried to strike hard at the evils which seem to me to lessen the power of the ministry in England; I have tried to strike hardest at the evils which have lessened the power of my own ministry. If these are evils which the students at Yale have no reason to fear, let them be thankful. If I had a larger knowledge of the Churches and of the ministry of the United States, I have sufficient faith in American generosity to believe that I should have given no offence had I attempted to discuss the special duties and dangers of the American preacher, as they appear to the eye of an Englishman. If any American minister would tell us English preachers, with perfect frankness, what he supposes to be our special defects and our special perils, we should receive his criticisms with cordial gratitude. But my knowledge of America did not justify me in making any such attempt.

I felt that the honour conferred upon me when I was invited to deliver these Lectures was so great that I was not at liberty to decline the invitation. I was bound to do what I could. The President and Fellows and Theological Faculty of Yale will, I trust, receive my assurance that if my power had been equal to my will I should have served them better.

R. W. DALE.

Birmingham.

CONTENTS.

LECTURE I.
INTRODUCTORY: PERILS OF YOUNG PREACHERS ... PAGE 1

LECTURE II.
THE INTELLECT IN RELATION TO PREACHING 27

LECTURE III.
READING 63

LECTURE IV.
READING (CONCLUDED) 90

LECTURE V.
THE PREPARATION OF SERMONS 116

LECTURE VI.
EXTEMPORANEOUS PREACHING AND STYLE 151

LECTURE VII.

EVANGELISTIC PREACHING 182

LECTURE VIII.

PASTORAL PREACHING 221

LECTURE IX.

THE CONDUCT OF PUBLIC WORSHIP: CONCLUSION ... 263

LECTURE I.

INTRODUCTORY: PERILS OF YOUNG PREACHERS.

GENTLEMEN,—My first duty is to express to the Theological Faculty and to the President and Fellows of this University my sense of the honour they have done me in nominating and appointing me to this lectureship. The illustrious services which Yale has rendered to the intellectual activity and culture of America, and the eminent learning of the long succession of its graduates and professors, might have made me shrink from accepting the distinction; but to have refused it would have been an ungracious return to your courtesy and kindness.

When I received the invitation to deliver this course of lectures, you had recently completed the centenary of your national independence. Perhaps that celebration may have made you more vividly conscious than ever that, although the political ties which once united the States of this great Republic to the ancient monarchy of England are severed, Americans and Englishmen still belong to the same race. It may have reminded you that the most heroic and glorious periods in the political history of the English people, the noblest names in our literature, the most sacred traditions of our Churches, are yours as well as ours. It may have renewed and deepened your generous affection for us. Gentlemen, I believe that every patriotic American and every patriotic Englishman, every wise and thoughtful Christian man on the other side of the Atlantic as well as on this, desires to draw closer and to strengthen those ties between the intellectual and religious life of the two countries, which the disruption of former political relations could not dissolve; and it is partly because I share this desire that I am here to-day.

In preparing these lectures, one consideration greatly relieved the anxiety from which it was impossible that I should altogether escape. I remembered that when you come to England you come to see the monuments and memorials of ancient life and manners. You care very much more for the cathedrals at Canterbury, Lincoln, and York, than for the new Houses of Parliament at Westminster. The Warwickshire lanes in which Shakspeare courted Ann Hathaway three hundred years ago, lanes with hedges which are as green to-day as they were in Shakspeare's time, and in which the same wild roses were growing last summer that he picked to make a wreath for her hair, are more attractive to you than the best railway line in the country; and to you, Shakspeare's house at Stratford-on-Avon is more interesting than any of the splendid mansions built for successful merchants and stockbrokers at South Kensington or Knightsbridge. Nor is your interest wholly absorbed in those ancient buildings which are attractive for their stately and noble architecture, or in those places which have the charm of association with famous names. Rude cottages by the roadside, or on village greens, cottages in which successive generations of obscure peasants have lived and died, and in which hardly a beam or a stone has been changed since the time of the Commonwealth; sleepy country towns lying remote from railways, and almost untouched by the life and stir of the present century; these also interest you, for at home you have nothing old except the rocks, the mountains, the stars, and the sea.

This seems to me to explain why an Englishman was nominated to this lectureship. Freshness, originality, brilliance—these the Theological Faculty and Corporation of Yale could find in abundance in this country. An Englishman was sent for, that for once you might have the opportunity of listening to lectures containing nothing fresh, nothing that should have the look of novelty, nothing but what had been familiar to men for hundreds of years, nothing but what was trite and commonplace.

And, gentlemen, I am increasingly disposed to value the trite and the commonplace, especially in everything that relates to the practical ordering of life and the securing of the great ends of human existence. With Nathaniel Culverwel, I always "reverence a grey-headed truth." When a truth comes to me which has been reasserted year after year for centuries, it comes with the sanction and authority, not of an individual man, but of successive generations of men. Our time in this world is too short for experiments the issue of which is uncertain. In the great affairs of life we can afford to risk nothing. It is as if we were making our way across a mountainous and perilous country, through which we had never travelled before: we are bound to reach the distant hospice on the other side of the great pass before the darkness sets in. We cannot venture on doubtful and unknown paths. Here is the well-beaten track under our feet; let us keep to it. It may not be quite the shortest way; it may not take us through all the grandeur and sublimity which bolder pedestrians might see; we may miss a picturesque waterfall, a remarkable glacier, a charming view; but the track will bring us safe to our quarters for the night. Yes, I repeat that in all that affects the supreme objects of life, I believe in the trite and the commonplace; and anyhow, just as in directing a stranger among the hills we feel obliged to point out to him the regular path, even though we ourselves might venture now and then to get away from it, so in giving advice to others we should be very cautious how we diverge from the conclusions which have been established by long experience and the general consent of wise men.

It is no part of my duty to say anything about your general studies. But you will allow me to express the earnest hope that you have so caught the enthusiasm for intellectual pursuits which ought to characterise a great university like this, that it is impossible for you to find without regret how rapidly session after session is drifting away, and how soon your studies in this place will be over. Never again, gentlemen, will you have such days of unbroken leisure for sustained and persistent intellectual work as you have now. Nor can the freshness and genial excitement of your student life ever return. In the soul's early admiration of the great achievements of human genius there is all the passion and joy and romance of first love; and the consciousness of the capacity for appreciating them is the verification of our own intellectual kinship with theologians, philosophers, poets, and orators, whose thought and passion have given life and strength and security to nations. There are none of us that have reached the iron age of conflict with the stubborn evils which afflict our race, who do not look back with something of sadness to the quiet, blessed years of our college life, the true golden age of our history.

But the heart of man is always restless, and I have no doubt that many of you are sometimes impatient for the days of energetic action which lie before you; and it is right that the thought of your future work should fill your heart, and that the earnest desire to be doing something towards lessening the sorrows and sins of men should occasionally master your intellectual enthusiasm. If, however, you are to be good preachers by-and-by, it is necessary that you should be hard students now. "For everything there is a season, and a time for every purpose under heaven." Impatience is not zeal. To despise present duties is not the way to prepare for duties yet to come. Self-conceit and intellectual indolence may sometimes disguise themselves under the form of eagerness to be preaching the gospel of Christ. Your life at the university is not merely a decent path to the ministry, but a preparation for it; and your future strength and success will be largely determined by the intensity of your devotion to the pursuits which claim—not your time and labour merely—but your very soul, within these walls.

You are Christ's servants—His "slaves," to use the title by which St. Paul delighted to describe himself. The work He has given you to do just now is your university work. Morning by morning, when the class-bell rings, "the tale of bricks" should be ready. You may sometimes find your work wearisome, and may be ready to think it unprofitable. There is nothing cheerful and exciting in Hebrew paradigms. The intricacies of the Gnostic heresies may sometimes seem very dull. But if you think that Christ meant you to come to the university, you must also think that He meant you to do the work of the university heartily. For a student to be careless in getting up his Hebrew verbs, or the chapters set him in Church history, is a sin; just as it is a sin for a preacher to be careless in preparing a sermon. Whatever work a Christian man does, is work that has to be done for Christ; and if we are negligent in the doing of it, we ought to confess our sin with sorrow and shame, and to ask Christ's forgiveness.

You ought also to remember that for purposes of intellectual discipline, a study which repels you is invaluable. If a professor found among his students a man who followed with equal eagerness every subject included in the ordinary scheme of studies, I am inclined to think that it would be the professor's duty to discover for that student's special benefit a subject that he would find offensive and intolerable. It is the very intention of a university course to enable a man to read—not what he likes, but what he does not like; to develop—not those intellectual muscles which are already healthy and vigorous, but those which are so weak that the slightest strain upon them is unwelcome while it lasts and leaves pain behind. Throughout life it is a wise practice to have always on hand two very different kinds of intellectual work —work which is a pleasure to us, for in that direction probably our true strength lies; and work which is a trouble to us, for by *that* our intellectual defects will probably be modified and corrected. Be thankful for the studies which are a drudgery to you ; never evade them, or, to use a fitter word—I do not know whether it is in use in America—never "scamp" them. They will give you what will be one of the chief elements of your power by-and-by, a despotic control over all your intellectual faculties, which will enable you to compel them to do their work, and to do it thoroughly, when they are most disposed to rebel.

I trust that, without giving offence to the learned professors who have charge of other departments, I may be permitted to utter an earnest and emphatic protest against the disposition to speak disparagingly and contemptuously of dogmatic theology—the very queen of the sciences. The mere intellectual interest of this regal study should protect it against dishonour. The gradual development, through successive generations, of vast theological systems is at least as noble an object of investigation as the gradual formation of the material world beneath our feet. These systems have also their *fauna* and their *flora*, and perpetuate the memory of types of human life and thought— some of them beautiful, some of them terrible, some of them grotesque—which have now quite disappeared. You will find in them the craters of extinct volcanoes, which once poured out rivers of flame and clouds of smoke that darkened the very heavens. They have had their glacier periods and their periods of torrid heat. The history of the evolution of the Calvinistic theory of the Divine government during the ages that lie between Augustine and Francis Turretin is quite as remarkable as the history of the formation of the tertiary strata ; and a sentence of the Athanasian creed, with the impress upon it of the subtle theories and protracted controversies from which it derived its precise form, is quite as curious a subject of study as a remarkable fossil in the limestone. Nor can we use the commonest theological terms intelligently without a knowledge of the roots from which they sprang— roots lying, some of them, far away in the obscure but daring speculations of Alexandria, and others in the philosophical systems of ancient Greece. For the very words of the great moral sciences are living things; they are not an artificial manufacture, like the technical terms of the physical sciences; they have come from the very life and soul of man; they tell the story of the deepest thoughts and most tragic struggles of the race, of its sins and its sanctity, its darkest fears and its divinest hopes. Nor can those who sneer at theology, if they think at all on the relations of the human soul to God, escape the necessity of finding some answer to the questions which theology attempts to solve, even if the only answer is that the questions are insoluble. And, for my part, I refuse to concur in the confession—very lightly and flippantly made by some men—that the subjects included in the range of theological science are inaccessible to us. Made in the image of God, with the history in our hands of a wonderful revelation of God to our race, and with the Spirit of God permanently abiding in the Church, we may know something of the nature of God and of His moral relations to mankind.

But the very craving for knowledge of this kind and the necessity of satisfying it will expose some of you to a serious peril. You will enter upon your ministry with many of the largest and deepest theological problems unsolved. Montesquieu said: "Il faut avoir beaucoup étudié pour savoir peu,"[1] which, being freely translated, amounts to this—that in order to know nothing, it is necessary that a man should have

[1] " Pensées Diverses."

studied a great deal. This is especially true in relation to philosophy and theology. When we begin we seem to know everything ; when we have been at work for three or four years we are confounded by discovering how much that we thought we knew has vanished. In these times, at least, however it may have been fifty years ago, a theological student who has any intellectual activity is sure to find that when his theological course is over his theological studies have only just begun.

Your faith in the Lord Jesus Christ, as God manifest in the flesh, may be strong and deep ; you may worship Him from your very heart ; His will may be your supreme law and His glory your supreme end ; you may rely upon Him with habitual and unfaltering confidence as the very fountain of spiritual light and life and strength ; and yet you may be unable for a long time to determine whether the Creed commonly known as the Creed of Athanasius defines accurately the eternal relations of the eternal Son of God to the eternal Father, or whether those relations have been more accurately defined by any modern theologian. You may be uncertain whether the Divine Person who became incarnate in Christ is rightly spoken of as having been the Son of God before the incarnation. While confessing His eternal and proper Deity, and acknowledging that "in Him were all things created that are in heaven and that are in earth, visible and invisible, whether they be thrones, or dominions, or principalities, or powers : all things were created by

Him and for [εἰς, unto] him;" you may hesitate to acknowledge the absolute equality of the eternal Son or the eternal Word to the Father, and may be disposed to believe that in the mysterious life of the Trinity there are relations of supremacy and subordination.

Questions of a different kind may remain for a time unsettled. You may be unable to form a conception of the relations between the Divine personality of the Lord Jesus Christ and His humanity, which shall seem consistent with the limitations of His knowledge, the development of His human perfection, and His accessibility to temptation.

There are other questions relating to the Lord Jesus Christ for which you may find it difficult to discover any satisfactory solution. Is the Lord Jesus Christ in any real sense the root of the whole human race? Is there in all men, as the result of their natural union with Him, a higher life, which is their true light? Does this life reveal itself in those that refuse to believe in Christ as well as in those that believe in Him? Does it reveal itself in heathen as well as in Christian lands? Is it in all men the source of moral intuitions which, however faint and however obscure, bear witness to the authority of the eternal law of righteousness? Is it in all men the source of thoughts which "wander through eternity," and of yearnings for the infinite and unknown, yearnings which, however vague and however ineffectual, are the invincible proof that the human race is akin to God? Or, on the other hand, is the

Divine life wholly absent from those who are not in the highest sense "in Christ," as the result of their personal faith in Him?

You may also be unable for a long time to construct any theory on the relation between the death of the Lord Jesus Christ and human redemption. You may believe that the death of the Lord Jesus Christ was an expiation for human sin, that it is the objective ground on which God forgives the sins of men; but what relation there is between His death and the Divine forgiveness you may be unable to discover. To discover it you will have to investigate the relation between the Divine Will and the Eternal Law of Righteousness, and between the Lord Jesus Christ and the race for which He died; and you will have to determine the nature of punishment, and the unique character of the Divine act which we describe as the remission of sins.

It is possible that before you leave this university you may have arrived at definite conclusions on some of these great and difficult theological problems; but if you have settled them all, and if you begin your ministry with your theological system completely developed, there must be a vast and inexplicable difference between the present position of theological speculation in America and in England. I believe that no such difference exists. The disorganisation of the older systems of theological thought is as complete among you as among us; the work of reconstruction is no farther advanced on this side of the Atlantic than on the other; the theological students of Yale have the same perplexities and uncertainties as the theological students of the old country; and you will have to begin to preach while the great task of organising your theological theories is still unfinished.

In England some young preachers transfer the process of constructing their systematic theology from the study to the pulpit; some young preachers in America may commit the same mistake. A friend of mine who had just left college said to me a few weeks ago, "A minister, when he is just beginning to preach, *must* sometimes write a sermon to clear his own mind on a subject." But a sermon which is written to "clear the mind" of the preacher will be very likely to perplex and confuse the minds of the hearers. It would strike you as very odd if a politician told you that he had made a speech in Congress in order to clear his own mind on the true economical doctrine about "hard money" and a paper currency: you would say that he ought to be sure about the doctrine before he prepared his speech.

If you are trying to settle any grave and important theological question, let your investigations be carried on in your study. You may do well to write as you think, for we very often discover that an argument, a conception, a theory, which seemed vigorous and beautiful in its disembodied form, becomes incoherent and wholly unsatisfactory as soon as it is fixed in words and transferred to paper. But say nothing till you have something to say. Even when we have reached a conclusion which seems satisfactory, it does not follow that we should make known our discovery in our next sermon. Delay will enable us to revise our position in new moods, and with an impartiality which is hardly possible when our discovery is quite fresh. It sometimes happens that what satisfies us perfectly on a bright wholesome morning in early autumn, looks very much less satisfactory on a foggy chilly day six weeks later. Or we find on reflection that some elements of the problem which ought to have been taken into account have been overlooked, and that our theory requires some slight modification; or that we had not quite seen all the relations between the new doctrine and other provinces of truth with which we had been long familiar, and that the lines defining the new territory have to be shifted here and there, and redrawn, in order to prevent encroachment on established rights.

There are other reasons for delay. In the first moment of discovery there is a certain intellectual exultation and pride on account of our achievement. We are apt at such a time to give ourselves airs, as though we too could now claim rank among original thinkers and among the reformers of theological science. We shall do well to give ourselves time to cool, and to recover our humility and modesty by remembering the vast and boundless regions which still lie beyond the limits of our thought. It is well to be cautious. Vauvenargues warns us that when we take the trouble to work out what strikes us as a profound discovery, we sometimes find that it is a truth known to every man we meet in the streets;[1] and sometimes what a young theologian receives with trembling wonder as a revelation fresh from heaven, never known before to scholar or saint, turns out to be one of those familiar elements of faith which every devout old lady in his congregation has known for years.

There is still another reason for delay when we think we have a grasp of new truth. We shall not be able at once to do justice to our new discovery. At first we shall not handle it firmly and with any freedom. The kind of mastery over a doctrine which is absolutely necessary to effective exposition can only come when by repeated and prolonged meditation we have made it perfectly familiar to us. Let me recommend you, therefore, to build up your theology in private, and not to perplex your congregations with speculations which are only half finished, with theories which are in process of formation. Let the walls of the building be dry before you ask people to come and live in it. Even when you think you have made sure of a new truth, or have constructed a more complete and philosophical exposition of a truth already acknowledged, do not be in a hurry to preach it. There is no need for being in a hurry. Do not be afraid that some one will get out a patent before you. The world

[1] "Lorsqu'une pensée s'offre à nous comme une profonde découverte, et que nous prenons la peine de la développer, nous trouvons souvent que c'est une vérité qui court les rues."— "Réflexions et Maximes."

can wait for your discovery a week or two longer after waiting for it through so many centuries; and perhaps the delay of even a few months will do mankind no great harm.

While the process of reconstructing your own theology is going on, you will be tempted to criticise with unsparing severity the traditional theology of evangelical Churches. Some of you will find that the temptation will be very strong. When a young man begins to preach, if he has any fervour in him, any enterprise, any intellectual brightness or freedom, he is very likely to think that the changes which are necessary in the thought of the Church are almost infinite.

> "Of old things all are over old,
> Of good things none are good enough,
> He'll show that he can help to frame
> A Church of better stuff." [1]

There are false conceptions of God, and of the ways of God to men; false conceptions of duty, and of the ideal of the Christian character. Doctrines which he supposes are commonly accepted seem to him illogical, unphilosophical, perhaps immoral, perhaps grotesque, perhaps blasphemous. Rules of life having wide authority, and regarded with ancient reverence, seem miserably artificial. What can he do? He does not know very much more than other people about positive truth. If it occurred to him to write down the truths of which he has made sure, and about which

---

[1] Wordsworth: "Rob Roy's Grave." I have taken some liberties with the original.

ordinary Christian people are either ignorant or mistaken, he would not want many sheets of foolscap to record them all. About how the facts really stand in relation to many great questions he is very uncertain: he is searching for truth, and in many directions he knows that he has not found it. He is acquainted with a great many speculations which have broken down, but as to the real truth about the subjects which these speculations were intended to illustrate and explain, he has not made up his mind.

But if he is not clear as to the right solution of many large and vital controversies, he is perfectly clear that the people about him have received by tradition very wrong solutions; and so he attempts to set them right. And yet this is hardly an accurate account of the matter: he shows them that they are wrong at present; but setting them right is a very different business. He smites the errors of the Church a little harder perhaps than the errors of the world. He thinks that in this way he shall get some sympathy for the Christian faith from those who have hitherto rejected it. He repeats in another form the mistake which is committed by politicians when they deliver speeches which are more loudly cheered by their opponents than by their own party. Politically, that style of speaking does not prove in the long run to have been very sagacious. It is much easier to lose friends than to gain opponents. The young preachers I am thinking of find this out in time. Meanwhile they go on confuting the errors of old-fashioned Christian people, and chaffing them for their narrowness and want of enlightenment. It is a delightfully easy occupation, and very exhilarating. It takes nothing out of a man. It is play, not work. Yet while a man is doing it he seems to be getting on wonderfully fast, and to be accomplishing amazing reforms.

Churches must bear with all this as patiently as they can, if the young preacher is right at heart, if it is clear that, with some intellectual waywardness and uncertainty, he really grasps the central truths of the Christian faith, and that notwithstanding some conceit he really wants to glorify God, and has only made a mistake about the best way to do it. He will find out his blunder in a few years. He will discover that, while perhaps he has been cutting up many weeds, he has planted very few trees and sown very little corn ; so that as autumn after autumn goes by, there is not much fruit ripening in the orchard and there is hardly any crop in the fields. He will discover that it is one thing to show men that they are in the wrong, and to leave them there—another thing to show them how to get right. He will ask himself, not how many errors he can confute, but how much positive truth he has to teach.

Gentlemen, would it not be well to ask yourselves that question before you enter the ministry? Before you begin to teach others, is it not desirable that you should know something yourselves? "We believe and therefore speak," has been the device of the true ministers of the Church from apostolic times to our own. Judging from many sermons which are preached in our day, there are ministers who have taken a new motto—" We disbelieve and therefore speak." But what results can come from a ministry which is almost wholly critical and destructive? What nobleness of moral character can it build up? What moral strength can it inspire? What ardour can it kindle? What lofty hopes can it confirm? What broken heart can it bind up? To what weariness can it give rest? What defence can it offer to the tempted? What relief from the consciousness of guilt to the penitent? What guidance to the soul that is athirst for the living God?

Have you anything to tell men that will make heaven seem nearer to earth than it ever was before, that will compel them to feel the tragic grandeur of human life and the infinite contrast between righteousness and sin? Have you anything to tell them which will save them from the bitterness of despair in their worst sorrows, and which will keep them calm and enable them to exercise self-restraint in their greatest successes and triumphs? Have you anything to tell them that, in the fiercest heat of youthful passion, under the severest strain of business and professional anxiety, and when the cold selfishness of old age is creeping upon them, will enable them to master the world, the flesh, and the devil? You are to be ministers of Christ —have you anything to say that ought to make the authority of Christ more awful and august to the conscience and the will, and the mercy of Christ more tender to the heart, of every man that listens to you? If not, then, whatever comes of it, refuse to be a candidate for a pulpit, refuse to accept the pastorate of a Church. Go down to New York, and work in the docks, or to Chicago, and get employment in the lumber trade; go out west and cultivate a farm, edit a newspaper, turn lawyer, become a clerk in a store or a hired waiter in an hotel; do anything to earn an honest living, but in God's name do not become a minister.

I have warned you against the mistake of those preachers who carry on in their sermons the intellectual labour of building up their own scientific theology, and of the mistake of those preachers who pass their time in the pulpit in the intellectual amusement of destroying the theological creed of other people. It is possible to avoid both these mistakes, and yet to miss the true end of preaching. While you are at the university you ought to be possessed with an ardent enthusiasm for intellectual pursuits, and it will be a great calamity if that enthusiasm is extinguished when you enter upon your ministry; but if you are to preach to any purpose you must care more for men than for learning and literature. There are some ministers who think so much about their sermons that they never seem to think about their congregations. They have so intense an intellectual delight in the exposition and defence of religious truth, that they do not remember that their business is to teach, to impress, to convert the living men and women that listen to them. If this does not happen often, it may be regarded as a venial offence. I do not think that any man preaches well whose purely intellectual interest in his work is not keen and strong. When the intellectual excitement of the preacher is passionate, it becomes contagious; the people catch it, and follow him from point to point with eager sympathy and interest.

In establishing the true sense of a perplexed passage of Holy Scripture by which many commentators have been baffled, in constructing a philosophical defence of some fundamental article of the Christian faith, in elaborating an exact definition of a great doctrine, in developing a theological theory, in destroying some ingenious and popular objection to the trustworthiness of revelation, in analysing the subtleties of some form of Christian experience, in discussing an important question of Christian ethics, it will do no harm if now and then we are so mastered by intellectual excitement as to forget the people to whom we are preaching. Occasionally it may do a congregation good to have their logical faculties strained to the utmost limits of endurance, like the muscles of a horse in a great race, and their whole intellectual life stirred to its very depths, by the defence, the demonstration, or the exposition of a great truth.

But never to think of the people to whom we have to speak, to forget them always, to preach Sunday after Sunday without any sympathy with their sorrows and disappointments, their happiness, their hopes, their struggles with temptation, their failures and their triumphs; to preach as though we were not of the same flesh and blood as our hearers, to permit our whole interest to be absorbed in the investigations of scholars and the controversies of theologians, to care less for the righteousness and the religious strength and joy of our congregations than for the beauty and depth of our thought, the grace and vigour of our style —this is treachery both to the Church and to Christ.

A year or two ago I heard two sermons while I was at the sea for my summer holiday. The preacher was a cultivated man, with an active, intelligent mind, and genuine religious faith. The prayers which he offered were true prayers, and would have made the service worth attending, had there been no preaching at all. The sermons were, of their kind, exceptionally good. The exegesis was sound and scholarly; the thought was ingenious and fresh; the illustrations were admirable; the style had only one fault—it was at times too delicately beautiful. But it did not seem to occur to the preacher that there was anybody listening to him. The sermons seemed to have been written simply because he found it pleasant to think and to write about the two texts which suggested them. I could not make out what truth he wanted to make clearer to us; or what neglected duty he wished us to discharge; or what devout affection he intended to quicken; or even what error he intended to expose.

Perhaps it may be said that sermons of this kind fall in with the mood and the habits of people who are away from home for rest. All the week long they are lying on the sands, listening to the dreamy music of the rising or the falling tide, and watching the changing lights on the sea; or they are wandering without any definite purpose over the hills; or reading idle books in shady glens; and on Sundays they are hardly prepared to listen to strenuous preaching. A quiet, thoughtful, devout meditation, with no particular object in it, is all they care for; and I admit that such sermons may be a pleasant change both to ministers and congregations, even when they are at home. I am afraid, however, that they are preached too often.

It seems hardly courteous, to say the least, to keep people listening to you for half-an-hour without considering whether what you are saying is likely to interest them or not. Congregations soon discover that their presence is not recognised by the minister, and they will leave him to do as well as he can without them. If a minister forgets that he has to preach to a congregation, the chances are that he will soon have no congregation to preach to.

Alexander Vinet reminds us that "preaching is an action."[1] A true sermon is meant to do something. It is not intended to be listened to merely. It fails of its purpose unless its makes some truth clearer, or more vivid, or more certain to those who hear it; or unless it explains and enforces some duty; or unless it strengthens some Christian affection; or brings solace to trouble, or courage to despondency. On Sunday evening, as we walked backwards and forwards on the sands, I ventured to tell my friend, whose sermons I have described, that it would do him a world of good

---

[1] "Pastoral Theology" (Clark's translation), p. 173.

to make twenty or thirty speeches at ward meetings, held night after night, in a hot municipal contest. If he had to persuade discontented ratepayers that the School Board had not spent too much on the school buildings, or paid the masters and mistresses too well ; or if he had to convince them that it would be worth their while to have the streets better paved, better swept, and better lighted ; that the health of the town would be improved if the corporation spent more money in removing nuisances ; that a scheme for a new street would soon repay the capital spent upon it ; if he had to expose the misrepresentations, correct the figures, demonstrate the groundlessness of the fears of the hostile party, and so to carry the vote and fire the zeal of meeting after meeting for his own candidate ; I thought that he might learn some lessons about preaching worth knowing. "To carry the vote and fire the zeal" of our congregations—this, gentlemen, is our true business. If we are to be successful there must be vigorous intellectual activity, but it must be directed by a definite intention to produce a definite result. Our intellectual activity must be of the nature of work—not merely of the nature of pleasant and healthy exercise. There must be patient instruction, solid argument, earnest appeal, declamation if you please ; but we must know what we mean to do, and we must put out our whole strength to get it done. We shall preach to no purpose unless we have a purpose in preaching. Archbishop Whately said of some preacher that "he aimed at nothing, and hit it."

But preaching may seem to be very effective, may attract great crowds, may produce intense excitement, may win for the preacher a wide reputation, and may yet be practically worthless and even mischievous. We cannot altogether escape the spirit of our times. When sensuous poetry is corrupting the public taste ; when coarse, sensational fiction is popular, not only among half-educated boys and girls, but among women who claim to have cultivation and refinement ; it is only natural that we should be in danger of adopting a melodramatic and hysterical kind of preaching, which stimulates the passions, but conveys no solid instruction and produces no wholesome moral or religious results.

I believe in the duty of consecrating to the exposition and defence of Divine truth every faculty and resource which the preacher may happen to possess. There is no power of the intellect, no passion of the heart, no learning, no natural genius, that should not be compelled to take part in this noble service. The severest and keenest logic, the most exuberant fancy, the boldest imagination, shrewdness, wit, pathos, indignation, sternness, may all contribute to the illustration of human duty and of the authority and love of God. If the heavens declare God's glory, if fire and hail, snow and vapour, and the stormy wind fulfil His word, if all His works praise Him, then the loftiest heights of intellectual majesty, the most dazzling intellectual splendours, every brilliant constellation in the firmament of genius, the lightnings and tempests of noble and eloquent passion, may also praise the Lord and show forth His excellent greatness.

But the mere sensational preacher cannot shelter himself under any such plea as this. He is always straining for excitement; he cares nothing about the means by which he produces it. Even if he has true genius his preaching is a peril to the souls of men. Dramatic power in the pulpit as well as on the platform or the stage may move to laughter or tears; impassioned rhetoric, when used by the religious orator as well as by the politician, may lash the most sluggish nature into vehement agitation; and a sermon, by the native force of the preacher, may produce an effect upon the emotions which may be mistaken for penitence, adoration, or faith. But if the effect which we produce is not produced by the clearness and energy and earnestness with which we illustrate the very truth of God, we shall save neither ourselves nor them that hear us. Most commonly the men who are tempted to preach in this style are mere charlatans. They have neither the fire of human genius nor the fire of a Divine zeal. They win a transient popularity, but they inspire no intellectual respect, they command no lasting confidence; their popularity is a shame to the Church, and contributes nothing to the final triumphs of the kingdom of God. I entreat you to refuse to purchase a temporary and worthless popularity by means so base. Preaching of this kind is a prostitution of the true dignity of the pulpit and a desecration of the gospel of Christ.

LECTURE II.

THE INTELLECT IN RELATION TO PREACHING.

GENTLEMEN,—It is my impression that some men of considerable intellectual resources and of genuine religious earnestness fail in the ministry and fail especially as preachers, through falling into habits which make them incapable of hard work. Indolence is a vice of which, perhaps, Americans are less likely to be guilty than Englishmen. There seems to be something in your climate, or in your national manners, or in the modification of your temperament since you came across the sea, which makes you alert, restless, and eager: among you the Anglo-Saxon sluggishness seems to have disappeared. But perhaps it will be wise not to be too sure of yourselves.

Are there no American ministers who were men of brilliant promise at the university, but who are most inefficient preachers?—none whom their friends describe as "unfulfilled prophecies"? Some men fail because they lose their spiritual earnestness; but others fail because in the course of a few years after they become pastors their intellectual force seems spent and their intellectual fire extinguished. Their sermons show no sign of elasticity and freshness of thought. The muscles of their mind have degenerated. If a preacher is to be effective—permanently effective—he must form and maintain habits of regular and strenuous intellectual activity, and he must exert his utmost intellectual strength in his sermons.

I do not mean that you should fill your sermons with antiquarian and historical and geographical learning. To do this may be sheer intellectual indolence. With the Bible Dictionaries and the books on the Geography and History of the Holy Land which are now accessible to us, a great show of learning may be made at the cost of a very little trouble. Even if hard work has been necessary to get the information together, no intellectual effort is required to transfer it from your note-book to your sermons. There are men who, if they are preaching on the Book of Exodus, will give you on one Sunday morning an elaborate account of the political and religious institutions of ancient Egypt. On the next they will confute the hypothesis that the pyramids near Cairo were built by the Jews during the evil times which followed the death of Joseph; perhaps they will describe the structure of the pyramids, and discuss the theory of Mr. Piazzi Smith as to the purpose for which they were erected; and they will be certain to say something about the probable sites of Pharaoh's "treasure cities—Pithom and Raamses." The Jews and their miseries will in all probability be quite forgotten, and no poor fellow in the congregation whose fortunes are ruined and whose heart is almost broken through the villainy of men whom he has trusted, or through the hardness and injustice of the men he is obliged to serve, will go home comforted because he has been reminded that God saw the affliction of His people in Egypt, and heard their cry, and knew their sorrows, and wrought great miracles for their deliverance. The next Sunday, when discoursing about the plagues, these preachers will say very little about the tragic interest of the conflict between the haughty king and the God whom he defied, about that persistent refusal to submit to God's authority which, in our own days and among ourselves, as in the days of Pharaoh, issues at last in a hardness of heart which makes repentance and salvation impossible; but they will speak learnedly about the natural history of Egypt, and about the natural phenomena of which the plagues were perhaps only the exceptional aggravation.

Even if they are preaching on the Gospels they will make no intellectual effort to bring vividly before you the Son of God in His living relations to the men and women that saw His face and heard His voice, and brought their children to Him to be healed of all kinds of diseases; but they will lazily repeat what they have read in Kitto, or Robinson, or Dean Stanley, or their Bible Encyclopædia, about the blue of Syrian skies, about the fertility of the plain of Gennesareth, about the range of limestone hills which form the backbone of Palestine, about the structure of Eastern houses, the family of Herod, the political condition of

Judæa and Galilee in the time of Christ, and the religious opinions of the Pharisees and Sadducees. Sermons of this sort are not at all of the kind that I am thinking of when I say that in your sermons you should exert your utmost intellectual strength. Such sermons as these may be written in your most indolent moods; you may write them on a hot summer's evening, when you are worn out with your year's work, and are longing for a holiday among the mountains or at the sea.

Nor am I asking you to try to preach what in England we are accustomed to call "intellectual" sermons. Some preachers are always "intellectual" and always cold. Their minds are never heated, even by the rapidity of their own movement. They seem incapable of passion,—even of what may be called intellectual passion. They put no more thought into their sermons than other men who have more fire; but because the thought is there and not the fire, they suppose that they are more "thoughtful" than their brethren. It would be just as reasonable to suppose that a skeleton in a surgeon's cupboard has more bones than a living man. The living man has quite as many bones as the skeleton; and besides the bones he has flesh and muscle; an eye that may be filled with sunshine or with tears; a voice that can command, or entreat, or comfort; a hand that can help or strike. The preachers that I am thinking of are satisfied with the "bones." When they have their "thought" they care for nothing more.

You do not suppose that because Burke's "French Revolution" is full of imagination, fancy, and fervour, there is less "thought" in it than in some essay on the Theory of Rent, which is hard logic from end to end; or that there is less "thought" in Shakespeare's "Tempest" and "King Lear" than in some dry and dreary dissertation on the doctrine of the Absolute. Burke and Shakespeare have as much "thought" as the political economist or the metaphysician, but the "thought" has flesh as well as bones, and is inspired by passion and imagination with a glorious life.

Your "intellectual" preachers are for the most part men who are destitute of some of the brightest and loftiest forms of intellectual power, or in whom they have been suppressed. These men may have worked hard in the forest, the quarry, and the mine; they may have prepared precious marbles, and silver ore, and gold of Ophir, and cedar trees and fir trees from Lebanon, for the house of their God; but the timber remains in rough logs, and the marble lies unpolished, and the costly metal has not been shaped into beautiful forms by the cunning hand of the artist. Why do they not finish their work? Is it because they are indolent? or is it because they have a false idea of what preaching ought to be? Or is it because they are mere quarrymen, and are destitute of the genius of the sculptor and the architect; have the strength to work hard at the gold diggings, but are incapable of mastering the art of the goldsmith? The intellectual activity which I ask for is the activity of all the various powers of your intellectual nature.

"Eloquence must be attractive," says Mr. Emerson. "The virtue of books is to be readable, and of orators to be interesting." He adds—and perhaps he is right —that "this is a gift of nature."[1] But there are men that have the "gift" who never use it in the pulpit. Let them speak at a political meeting, or, indeed, at a meeting of any kind, and their speeches are bright with fancy and warm with generous excitement; memory, wit, imagination, are all alert and active; they make the most felicitous quotations from ancient and modern poets; they remember wise and noble sentences in Plato, in Hooker, in Jeremy Taylor, in Pascal; they are familiar with Sir Walter Scott and with Nathaniel Hawthorne and with Charles Dickens; they have a humorous tale to tell which they have met with in some book of travels; or they remind you of a pathetic story which you saw in the newspaper the day before; or they have an adventure of their own to describe, and you are moved to laughter or tears. But let them once begin to preach, and everything is changed. One might almost imagine that between the vestry and the pulpit they had seen the sable throne of the goddess of the "Dunciad,"—

> "Before her, Fancy's gilded clouds decay,
> And all its varying rainbows die away.
> Wit shoots in vain its momentary fires,
> The meteor drops, and in a flash expires.

---

[1] "Society and Solitude." English reprint, p. 59.

>   As one by one, at dread Medea's strain,
>   The sickening stars fade off th' ethereal plain;
>   As Argus' eyes by Hermes' wand opprest,
>   Closed one by one to everlasting rest;
>   Thus at her felt approach, and secret might,
>   Art after art goes out, and all is night."

Or if it is hardly fair to say that the presence of the drowsy goddess sinks their whole intellectual life into slumber, this at least must be acknowledged, that three-fourths of their powers are in a condition of suspended animation from the moment they announce their text till the sermon is finished. At the very best there is an unnatural strain on the faculties which retain their activity, and which are compelled to do all the work—a strain which is felt by the preacher, and is felt still more by those members of the congregation who conscientiously endeavour to hear the sermon through. The same muscles are on the stretch all the time.

We ought to remember that for an ordinary speaker to excite and maintain the interest of his audience it is indispensable that he should appeal to various susceptibilities of emotion and bring into play various intellectual powers. Monotony is almost always fatal to interest; monotony of voice, monotony of style, monotony of intellectual activity. No doubt there have been great preachers whose names may be quoted against me. They achieved all their success by the manly breadth and strenuous vigour of their logic, or by the terrible vehemence with which they were able to denounce sin, or by their pathos, or by their imaginative fire, or by the keenness of their moral penetration. There was no variety of power; but the solitary power they had was of transcendent force, and great congregations listened to them without weariness. Such examples, however, count for nothing. These were extraordinary men; we are not. The chances are that we have no single faculty in such consummate vigour and perfection that we can rely on it for everything. We ought to take it for granted that we must use every resource we have, in order to be effective or even interesting.

Mr. Emerson's words are worth quoting again: "It is the virtue of orators to be interesting." I doubt whether preachers have any right to complain if people who used to come to church regularly get into the habit of staying away. If we were "interesting," they would find it pleasanter to listen to our sermons than to spend the morning at home, writing letters or reading the newspapers. I am sure that we have no right to complain if while we are preaching people go to sleep. It is our duty to keep them awake. Nor have we any right to complain that while they seem to be listening to us they are thinking of their farm, or their store, or the new flower they have got for their green-house, or the new horse they have bought for their carriage. If I were speaking to a congregation instead of to a class of students preparing for the ministry, I should, perhaps, tell them that they ought to make an effort to fix their minds on the sermon, and that they ought to drive away all thoughts that would distract their attention; but as I am speaking to *you*, I am bound to maintain that it is your business to make your sermons so interesting, that the people, so far from having to make an effort to think of what you are saying to them, shall have to make an effort to think of anything else.

Some of you, perhaps, had the good fortune to hear the late Mr. George Dawson lecture or preach when he was visiting the States, a year or two before his death. He was a speaker who charmed and delighted all kinds of audiences — literary men and farm-labourers, merchants and mechanics. He once said to me, "When I speak I make up my mind that the people shall listen to me: if they don't listen, it doesn't matter *what* you say." That is a maxim which it will be worth our while to remember, especially if we complete it by adding that "if the people do listen, what you say matters a great deal." The maxim is obvious enough, and yet there are preachers to whom it never seems to have occurred.

Perhaps I may be warned that if the kind of advice which I am giving you just now is followed, it will be likely to lower the dignity of the pulpit. Gentlemen, I decline to believe that dulness is necessary to dignity. The dignity of the pulpit is derived from the grandeur and glory of the truths which the preacher has to illustrate, and from the solemnity of the duties which he has to enforce; from the infinite issues which depend upon the manner in which the truths are received and the duties discharged by the people that listen to him; from the interest of God Himself in the varying fortunes of the conflict which the preacher is maintaining with the atheism, the irreligion, the evil practices, and the moral indifference of mankind; from the mysterious and supernatural forces which are in alliance with the preacher in this tremendous and protracted conflict — for while the preacher is speaking there is another voice than his appealing to the hearts and consciences of men, the voice of the Divine Spirit; and there is the invisible presence of Him who, when He charged His apostles to teach all nations what He had commanded them, declared that while they were fulfilling their commission He would be with them always, even to the end of the world. In an inferior degree the dignity of the pulpit is derived from the intellectual force and culture of the preacher, from his moral qualities, and from his personal sanctity; from his courage, his gentleness, his zeal, and from the earnestness and energy with which he uses all his powers to secure the triumph of righteousness, and the rescue of the human race from its sorrows and its sins. If there is any dignity derived from dulness, I care nothing for it. Dignity which is purchased at the expense of efficiency is dignity of a false and artificial kind. And, to return to the point from which I have wandered, we cannot be efficient if we are not interesting; nor can we be interesting if we suppress all those intellectual faculties which would give brightness, colour, variety, and animation to our preaching. Nor is it merely for the sake of stimulating and sustaining the interest of the people that I ask you to use, in the pulpit, all the intellectual powers you possess, and to take care that by your private reading these powers are kept in vigorous health and activity. You need them all if you are to preach efficiently.

Take what may be regarded by inconsiderate persons as the easiest part of our work—the mere statement and exposition of religious truth. It may be supposed that any one who has mastered a truth will be able to make it clear to other people. But a moment's reflection will convince you that this is a mistake. Is a man able to tell a story clearly and accurately merely because he knows all the facts? It often requires all the ingenuity and patience of a skilful barrister to draw out of a friendly witness an intelligible account of what the witness saw with his own eyes, heard with his own ears, and perfectly remembers. Mr. Huxley—you will forgive me, I am sure, for taking my illustrations from the other side of the Atlantic; I have too limited an acquaintance with distinguished Americans to enable me to appeal with any confidence in my accuracy to the names with which you are most familiar, and which would occur most naturally to an American minister occupying this chair—Mr. Huxley has, no doubt, immense scientific knowledge, and is also eminent as a keen and original observer of scientific phenomena, but he owes his distinction, partly, to his rare powers of exposition. To listen to one of his popular lectures is a lesson in rhetoric. Mr. Gladstone has an extraordinary genius for finance, but his power of making a financial statement is, perhaps, equally extraordinary. When he was Chancellor of the Exchequer his budget speech was always one of the great oratorical triumphs of the session. He often spoke for three hours, and the House of Commons was under a spell all the time. Of course, before our tariff was simplified by Mr. Gladstone's policy, the budget speech always excited a curiosity and interest of which the dullest Chancellor was able to avail himself. Every one wanted to know whether the expenditure for the year was to be provided for by loading the income tax with an additional penny, or whether the Chancellor was sufficiently well satisfied with what we became accustomed to call the natural expansion of other sources of revenue to take a penny off. Tea merchants and grocers were eager to learn whether the duty on tea was to be kept up; coffee merchants, whether the duty on coffee was to be lowered; sugar refiners, whether the sugar duties were to be touched; farmers, whether the Government was disposed to make any concessions to them in the matter of the malt tax. It required very little skill so to arrange the successive disclosures of the intentions of the Government as to keep the attention of the House active and awake to the very end of a long speech. But Mr. Gladstone used to develop his financial proposals with all the art with which a skilful novelist develops his plot. There were alternations of hope and fear. At the very moment when you expected that your eager curiosity would be satisfied, and that you would hear how everything was going to turn out, some new complication arose, of exciting interest, and you began to suspect that you were only half through the second volume of the story, instead of being at the end of the third. It was not merely in the way in which he kept all the commercial "interests" on the stretch that he showed his power. The statement of the revenue and expenditure for the past year had appeared in the morning newspapers, but when he went through the statement at night, and explained it to the House, the figures which you had seen a few hours before, printed in black ink, were full of life and light.

It was very wonderful, and showed what may be done by the power of skilful exposition, by an ingenious arrangement of topics, by stimulating curiosity before satisfying it, by making everything clear as you go along, and yet taking care not to exhaust the interest of your audience prematurely. A dull Chancellor, with the same materials before him, would have gone through the points in his "notes" just as they happened to come; would have given the explanation furnished by one of his subordinates of how it was that the customs or the excise exceeded or fell short of the calculations he had submitted twelve months before; would have reminded the House in a dreary way of the unexpected circumstances which had rendered necessary a larger expenditure on the army or the navy than had been provided for in the estimates for the preceding year; and would then have stated in a few brief sentences what taxes and duties he proposed to increase or to diminish. But a statement like this, though it might contain the whole substance of one of Mr. Gladstone's great speeches, might just as well be printed as spoken. It would require an intellectual effort to master the details. When they were mastered they would soon be forgotten. It was the merit of Mr. Gladstone's eloquence that it fascinated people to whom finance was intolerably dry and unattractive ; enabled them to understand, without any consciousness of painful intellectual exertion, details which in print would have had no meaning to them, and fixed the general financial position of the country in their memory.

It seems easy to tell others what we know ourselves, but this power of exposition is in reality a difficult òne for most men to acquire. I do not know that I can say anything about the way to acquire it which will be of much service to you, and my present object is merely to insist on its importance and value. The root of the power, I believe, lies in honest intellectual habits. Be sure that you know what you think you know. Instead of yielding too much to the passion for making your way into fresh and untravelled provinces of truth, make yourselves perfectly familiar with the truth you know already. Do not imagine that you know anything because you have a convenient formula in which you can express it. Get at the facts which lie behind the formula, and live among them.

Every subject on which we intend to speak should be in our complete possession *as a whole*, and not merely in its various parts. We must form the habit of keeping suspended before our own mind all that we have to say. I mean that we must not be satisfied with thinking in succession of the successive points which we intend to touch ; we must get the power of seeing all the points at once, and in this way we shall become familiar with the relations between them. This habit and faculty may be strengthened by patient and honest reading. Before beginning a book it is well to look carefully through the table of contents, and to learn all that we can about the general design of the author, the method he has followed, the relations between the various topics he has discussed, and the various arguments on which he has relied. After finishing the book we should repeat the process. We should look at the book as a whole, and piece together all its parts. When we are trying to master the geography of a country, we place vividly before our minds the mountains which run through it, and fix the watersheds : these determine the courses of the rivers. Then we picture to ourselves the outline of the coast. Then we distribute the mining districts. The physical features of the country suggest its natural political boundaries. The navigable rivers, the harbours, the mines, determine the sites where the great towns are naturally built ; and these again determine the principal lines of communication, the roads, the canals, and the railways. It is in this way, and only in this way, that we can get a complete and organic conception of the geography of a country, and we must adopt a similar method if we are to get a complete and organic conception of the contents of a book. Everything worth reading with any care may be treated in this way; an epic poem as well as a philosophical discussion; a tragedy as well as a theological argument; an impassioned lyric as well as a sermon; the story of a campaign as well as the decrees of a council and the articles of a confession of faith. If you acquire the power of grasping firmly and as a whole what other men have thought and written, you will find it far easier to grasp in the same way what you have thought and written yourselves; and this intellectual mastery of a subject is necessary to the clear and effective exposition of it.

That if you are to preach well you ought to keep your logical faculty bright and clear, is so obvious that I need hardly insist upon it. American preaching, I am told, is conspicuously argumentative. You "prove all things." But it may not be unnecessary to remind you that of all public speakers a preacher is most in danger of using arguments which prove nothing. He does not speak under the salutary restraints which compel other public men to consider whether there is any relation between their premises and their conclusions. There is no one to reply to him at the time, and the fear of the newspaper belonging to the other party is not before his eyes. This immunity from hostile discussion and criticism ought to lead us to be the more careful and conscientious in making sure of the soundness of our reasoning ; and since we are deprived of the logical discipline which comes from fair and open debate with equal opponents, we should subject ourselves to discipline of another kind.

The rules and exercises of formal logic are not without their value : to me they seem to afford an admirable method of intellectual training, and the contempt with which they are sometimes spoken of is extremely unwise and indefensible. But if you wish to invigorate your argumentative power, and to maintain habits of logical accuracy, let me advise you to try your strength against the great writers in various departments of thought, theology, philosophy, politics. Master their method of proof. Compel your mind to follow their reasoning step by step, and at every step make sure that the ground is firm. Beware of an indolent acquiescence in an argument on behalf of your own opinions. Keep your mind awake and active. Do not suffer yourselves to drift passively down the stream of any man's logic ; try whether the current is so strong that you cannot swim against it. Challenge every position maintained by your author. Test the strength of every link in his reasoning. Work of this kind will prevent your intellectual muscles from becoming flaccid. It will answer the purpose of practice with the foils: it will improve your " wind," give suppleness to your limbs, make your eye keen and your stroke sure.

If you are to preach effectively you must also

endeavour to keep your fancy fresh and your imagination active. Every lecturer on preaching, every writer on rhetoric, insists on the importance of "illustrations." They tell us that logic may lay the foundations and build the walls of the house, but that "illustrations" are the windows which let in the light. But I wish to remind you that if fancy is active and imagination vigorous, the walls will not merely be pierced with occasional windows—the walls themselves will be transparent, the light will come through everywhere.

I do not mean, of course, that it is a merit for a sermon to be overlaid with ornament. Mere ornament, instead of making our meaning clearer, is likely to conceal it, just as architectural decoration sometimes conceals the true lines of a building. It is not of ornament I am thinking, but of the firm and vigorous expression of our thought. All language representative of intellectual acts and moral qualities was created by the imagination, and every word that stands for a spiritual idea was at first a picture and a poem. The imaginative process, which in the earliest periods of human history transmuted the names of material things into the symbols of intellectual and spiritual attributes and activities, is going on perpetually. It is one of the distinctions of an original and powerful writer or speaker that his thoughts have sufficient life and vigour in them to form for themselves, out of the common air and the common earth, a visible organisation—" a spiritual body "—of their own.

De Quincey has some very striking observations on Edmund Burke which illustrate my meaning. In reply to those critics who are accustomed to speak of the fancy of Burke, he says, with his customary scorn of opinions which he rejects: " Fancy in your throats, ye miserable twaddlers! As if Edmund Burke was the man to play with his fancy for the purpose of separable ornament. He was a man of fancy in no other sense than as Lord Bacon was so, and Jeremy Taylor,[1] and as all large and discursive thinkers are and must be; that is to say, the fancy which he had in common with all mankind, and very probably in no eminent degree, in him was urged into unusual activity under the necessities of his capacious understanding. His great and peculiar distinction was that he viewed all objects of the understanding under more relations than other men, and under more complex relations.... Now to apprehend and detect more relations, or to pursue them steadily, is a process absolutely impossible without the intervention of physical analogies. To say, therefore, that a man is a great thinker, or a *fine* thinker [by which De Quincey has explained he means a *subtle* thinker], is but another expression for saying that he has a *schematising* (or, to use a plainer, but less accurate expression, a figurative) understanding. In that sense, and for

[1] Not having the fear of De Quincey's scorn to restrain me, I venture to say that the appeal to Jeremy Taylor seems unfortunate. Surely with him Fancy often usurped a place to which she had no claim, forgot that she was a subject, and reigned as a queen--a veritable Queen Mab of Fairyland.

that purpose, Burke is figurative; but understood, as he *has* been understood by the long-eared race of his critics, not as thinking in and by his figures, but as deliberately laying them on by way of enamel or after-ornament — not as *incarnating*, but simply as *dressing* his thoughts in imagery—so understood, he is not the Burke of reality, but a poor, fictitious Burke, modelled after the poverty of conception which belongs to his critics."[1]

You will observe that De Quincey says that Burke thought "in and by his figures." Imagination furnished him — not with mere jewellery for beauty and ornament — but with the very tools and instruments necessary to the process of thinking. In his case, according to De Quincey, the subtlety and originality of his thought imposed upon the imagination this service. The concrete symbols had to be created which were necessary to make definite and visible to himself the movements of his intellectual activity, and to fix their results. In our case it is probable that the symbols already formed to our hand by the creative genius of other men will be found sufficient for the purposes of our private thinking, and fancy will not be "urged into unusual activity under the necessities of a capacious understanding." But there will be all the more reason for keeping it active by other means. We may be able to think accurately in abstract terms, but if we are to speak vigorously, our thoughts must take form and

[1] De Quincey: "Rhetoric." Works. Vol. x. pp. 56, 57.

colour, must clothe themselves in flesh and blood, so that they can be seen and handled by the people who are listening to us. It may not be necessary to be constantly creating new imagery and new forms of expression to convey our meaning; if the common language of common men will serve our turn, we should use it.

As I have said, every word that stands for a spiritual idea was at first a picture and a poem. In the case of most words of this class, the image stamped upon them by the fancy of the poet has worn away and become undistinguishable, like the impression on a coin which has been passing from hand to hand for a generation:—the colours have faded from the canvas, and have left vague and blurred outlines where there was once a picture. If your imagination is vigorous, you will so use these words as to restore to the worn coin the sharpness of the original impression, and to the canvas the brilliance and the richness of the original colouring. The difference between vivid and languid speaking depends very largely upon the extent to which the imagination contributes in this way to the expression of thought. The imaginative speaker instinctively rejects words, phrases, symbols, which are incapable of being animated with vital warmth. He rejects them as a tree rejects withered leaves and dead wood. His style is alive in every fibre of it.

Imagination has another function which perhaps young preachers are in some danger of forgetting. In the investigation of truth we are anxious to work in the dry light of the logical understanding. We make it a matter of conscience to give to every argument its just weight, and not more than its just weight; to follow every line of evidence as far as it will legitimately lead us, and no farther. There is an intellectual integrity which to the scholar is everything that commercial integrity is to the merchant and judicial integrity to the judge. When men leave the university they are apt to suppose that the same laws which should govern the search for truth have authority in the propagation of it. They have a suspicion that their intellectual honesty will be compromised if they set an argument on fire with imagination and passion.

But imagination is a most legitimate instrument of persuasion. It is an indispensable instrument. The minds of men are sometimes so sluggish that we cannot get them to listen to us unless our case is stated with a warmth and a vigour which the imagination alone can supply. There are many, again, who are not accessible to abstract argument, but who recognise truth at once when it assumes that concrete form with which imagination may invest it; they cannot follow the successive steps of your demonstration, but they admit the truth of your proposition the moment you show them your diagram. Then, again, there are some truths—and these among the greatest—which rest, not upon abstract reasoning, but upon facts. Imagination must make the facts vivid and real.

Further—in a country like this there are large numbers of persons to whom it is unnecessary to offer any proof of the great articles of the Christian faith, although they are living in the habitual neglect of Christian duty. That there is a living God; that He abhors sin and loves righteousness; that the Lord Jesus Christ is the Son of God; that He died for them, and that He will come again to judge the living and the dead, they believe. But these awful and glorious truths, though they have a place in the intellect, exert no influence on the heart, the conscience, and the will. They inspire no wonder; they alarm no fear; they kindle no hope; they quicken no affection; they fail even to excite the faintest moral interest. All life has gone out of them. But imagination is akin to emotion—much nearer akin than the logical understanding—and in such cases imagination may do something to bridge the gulf between the speculative and the active powers; may fulfil the office which Bolingbroke attributes to history, and "set passion on the side of judgment, and make the whole man of a piece."

There are some verses in Mr. Tennyson's "In Memoriam" which remind us of another reason why the Christian preacher, above all other public speakers, should cultivate this faculty.

> " Though truths in manhood darkly join
> Deep-seated in our mystic frame,
> We yield all blessing to the name
> Of Him that made them current coin.

"For wisdom dealt with mortal powers,
  Where truth in closest words shall fail,
  When *truth embodied in a tale*
Shall enter in at lowly doors.

"And so the Word had breath, and wrought
  With human hands the creed of creeds,
  In loveliness of perfect deeds,
More strong than all poetic thought.

"Which he may read that binds the sheaf,
  Or builds the house, or digs the grave,
  And those wild eyes that watch the wave
In roarings round the coral reef."

Nor is it merely at "lowly doors" that "truth embodied in a tale" finds easier entrance than truth which appears in the form of abstract propositions. God, who knows as we cannot know the mystery of our nature, has revealed Himself to mankind in a supernatural history. The revelation which we have to illustrate, and which furnishes the very substance of all our preaching, is not a series of theological dogmas or ethical principles; it is in the main a record of how God has dealt with individual men, with nations, and with the human race. Above all, it is the story of the earthly life, the death, the resurrection, and the ascension into heaven of our Lord Jesus Christ—God manifest in the flesh.

What is commonly described as an historical imagination, is indispensable to us if we are to form a right judgment on the historical contents of Holy Scripture. "Our view of any transaction," says Archbishop Whately, "especially one that is remote in time or place, will necessarily be imperfect, generally incorrect, unless it embrace something more than the bare outline of the occurrences; unless we have before the mind a lively idea of the scenes in which the events took place, the habits of thought and of feeling of the actors, and all the circumstances of the transaction; unless, in short, we can in a considerable degree transport ourselves out of our own age and country and persons, and imagine ourselves the agents and spectators. . . . To say that imagination, if not regulated by sound judgment and sufficient knowledge, may chance to convey to us false impressions of past events, is only to say that man is fallible. But such false impressions are even *much the more* likely to take possession of one whose imagination is feeble or uncultivated."[1]

If the imaginative faculty is too sluggish to make the facts which are the vehicles of a large part of Divine revelation real and alive to us, we shall read two-thirds of the Old Testament and a third of the New with very languid interest; we shall fail to discover the truths and laws which the facts illustrate, and our hearts will remain untouched by the story. Even the epistles—and the epistles which are most exclusively doctrinal—will fail to convey to us their true meaning, unless we are able, by an effort of the imagination, to reproduce to ourselves the circumstances, the habits of thought, the moral and spiritual perils of the people to whom they were written, and

[1] Whately: "Rhetoric," p. 124.

the personal character and idiosyncrasies of the apostolic writers. If we are to understand the Epistle to the Galatians, we must become, while we read it, members of one of the Galatian Churches, with our minds imperfectly liberated from heathenism, and impressed by the confident claims of those who profess to be truer representatives of the new faith than St. Paul, from whom we first heard the gospel of Christ. We must know St. Paul as the Philippians knew him, and we must love him as they loved him, if we are to understand the Epistle to the Church at Philippi. There is hardly a page of Holy Scripture which will not become more intelligible to us if we read it with an active imagination.

And when we have discovered for ourselves what the Scriptures were intended to teach, we shall not, if we are wise, forget the form in which the teaching is given. The facts are still the most effective expression of the truths contained in them. The history of Joseph—of his slavery, his imprisonment, his rise to the government of Egypt—can never be made obsolete by any theories of Providence; nor the history of the sin and anguish of David by any theological argument demonstrating the necessity of repentance; nor the history of the catastrophes which came upon the Jewish race by any ethical proof of the certain ruin which God will inflict upon a nation that revolts against the authority of the moral law. The miracles of Christ are still the most pathetic evidence of God's compassion for human infirmity and suffering. The death of Christ is the final expression of the infinite love of God for all mankind.

As the truths which we have to teach concerning God are contained in the facts which constitute the chief part of God's revelation of Himself to our race, so the ethical and spiritual laws which should regulate the Christian life are most vividly illustrated in the virtues and the vices, the sanctity and the sins, of the men whose story has been preserved to us in the Jewish and Christian Scriptures. The preachers who have learnt how to use these ancient facts are in possession of a power which reaches the hearts and consciences of all sorts of men. You know how Mr. Moody uses them. He talks as though Jacob had been an intimate personal friend of his; as though he had met the patriarch near Bethel the morning after he had seen the vision of the ladder and the angels; had been with him when his cruel sons brought to his tent the coat of many colours dipped in blood; had seen the old man's face when in later years these same sons returned from Egypt and told him how roughly the governor had treated them, that he had charged them with being spies, that he had made them promise to bring Benjamin down into Egypt to verify their account of themselves, and that meanwhile he had kept Simeon as a hostage of their good faith. While you are listening to Mr. Moody you are ready to think that he must have been in the boat with the apostles when Christ came to them over the stormy sea; must have seen the lad who had the basket on his arm with the five barley loaves in it and the two small fishes; must have been at the wedding feast at Cana, and tasted the wine which came out of the waterpots. At times his realisation of the story he is telling becomes so intense that he almost makes you feel as though you as well as he had been in the upper chamber and listened to our Lord's last discourse to His disciples; had seen Him rise to go, and then linger, because He had not yet told them all that was in His heart; had gone with Him through the streets of Jerusalem and across the ravine of the Kedron, bright with the full moon, to the dark shadows of the olive trees of Gethsemane; had seen Him in His agony; had been startled by the appearance of Judas with the crowd that came to arrest Him; had followed Him afar off to the house of Caiaphas, and then to the judgment-hall of Pilate, and then to the palace of Herod; had stood at last under the walls of Jerusalem and watched Him as He hung on the cross, crowned with thorns; had been filled with terror by the earthquake and the darkness; and had heard Him cry with a loud voice, "Father, into thy hands I commend my spirit."

No doubt Mr. Moody makes the patriarchs and the apostles talk as though they had been born in Chicago. His reproduction of the ancient stories is wanting in exact historical truth, because the whole costume in which he clothes the characters is modern and western —not ancient and oriental. In fact, he translates the men themselves and their ways of thought and action into English, as the venerable scholars who produced our Authorized Version translated their mere words into English. In this respect I do not ask you to follow his example. With the knowledge of ancient life and manners which you have acquired in this university, it would be impossible, even if it were desirable, for you to follow it. But if you have any of that dramatic imagination which he possesses in so eminent a degree, you ought to learn from him the wisdom of cultivating it, for it is one of the principal elements of his power as a preacher.

Every intellectual faculty that contributes to the vivacity, keenness, and strength of the graver forms of secular eloquence, may also contribute to the efficiency of the Christian preacher. Not to appeal to the sermons of uninspired men, whose authority might be challenged, let us turn to the Holy Scriptures themselves. Examples of humour might be difficult to find, unless we admitted that it appears in a most cynical form in the Book of Ecclesiastes; but there is surely something like it in that delicious touch of St. Paul's in the Second Epistle to the Corinthians (Chap. xii. 12, 13). "Truly the signs of an apostle were wrought among you in all patience, in signs, and wonders, and mighty deeds. For what is it wherein *ye* were inferior to other churches, except it be that I myself was not burdensome to you? *forgive me this wrong.*" Irony, and irony which at times becomes scornful, he uses freely in both epistles. "Seeing that many glory after the flesh, I will glory also. For ye suffer fools gladly, seeing ye yourselves are wise" (2 Cor. xi. 18, 19). Again, "Who maketh thee to differ from another? and what hast thou that thou didst not receive? now if thou didst receive it, why dost thou glory, as if thou didst not receive it? Now ye are full, now ye are rich, ye have reigned as kings without us: and I would to God ye did reign, that we also might reign with you" (1 Cor. iv. 7, 8).

In the prophets, the idolatry into which the Jewish people were continually being betrayed is overwhelmed with the most bitter, contemptuous, and elaborate sarcasm. "Who hath formed a god, or molten a graven image that is profitable for nothing? . . . The smith with the tongs both worketh in the coals, and fashioneth it with hammers, and worketh it with the strength of his arms: yea, he is hungry, and his strength faileth: he drinketh no water, and is faint. The carpenter stretcheth out his rule; he marketh it out with a line; he fitteth it with planes, and he marketh it out with the compass, and maketh it after the figure of a man, according to the beauty of a man. . . . He heweth him down cedars, and taketh the cypress and the oak, which he strengtheneth for himself among the trees of the forest: he planteth an ash, and the rain doth nourish it. . . . He burneth part thereof in the fire; with part thereof he eateth flesh; he roasteth roast, and is satisfied: yea, he warmeth himself, and saith, Aha, I am warm, I have seen the fire: and the residue thereof he maketh a god, even his graven image: he falleth down unto it, and worshippeth it, and prayeth unto it, and saith, Deliver me; for thou art my god" (Isa. xliv. 10–17).

I decline to acknowledge the binding force of those traditions which deny to the Christian preacher the weapons which have been consecrated by the hands of Isaiah and St. Paul. A prudent man will of course be careful to remember the tastes and the habits of the people to whom he has to preach; and in congregations which have been long accustomed to the dignity of a dull propriety in the pulpit, a young minister will make it a matter of conscience to be dull; or, at least, he will avoid making his sermons too interesting and too attractive. If he asserted the perfect intellectual freedom which Christ has given us, but which the traditions of some pulpits refuse to allow, he would fail to secure the very results for which — and for which alone — he has to use all his intellectual resources. We cannot speak to men effectively of the "wonderful works of God" unless we speak to "every man in his own tongue wherein he was born." Congregations which have not been accustomed to the play of humour and fancy, to the glow of a fervid imagination, to the keen edge of sarcasm, will be perplexed and alarmed if sermons have too much intellectual vivacity in them. I say that they will be alarmed as well as perplexed: they will not only fail to recognise familiar truth in its unfamiliar form; they will be shocked at what they will regard as the secularisation of the pulpit. It is still true that "one believeth that he may eat all things:

another, who is weak, eateth herbs." To the weak we may say, "Let not him which eateth not, judge him that eateth.... Who art thou that judgest another man's servant? to his own master he standeth or falleth. Yea, he shall be holden up, for God is able to make him stand." But to the strong we must also say, "Let not him that eateth despise him that eateth not.... I know, and am persuaded by the Lord Jesus, that there is nothing unclean of itself.... But if thy brother be grieved with thy meat, now walkest thou not charitably. Destroy not him with thy meat, for whom Christ died." Charity is the supreme law of Christian rhetoric as well as of the Christian life.

"If meat make my brother to offend, I will eat no flesh while the world standeth;" and the preacher who happens to be a man of genius, will say: To me it may seem that glorious truth should clothe herself in the glorious robes of imagination, and be crowned with the flowers of fancy; that in her gentler reproofs a pleasant irony may play on her lips; and that in her anger, indignation may flash from her eye, and the lightnings of a fierce sarcasm may be hurled by her hand. But if imagination, fancy, irony, and sarcasm make my brother to offend, I will become a fool for Christ's sake, and will be dull while the world standeth.

To this severity of intellectual asceticism, however, I believe that none of us are called. It is very rarely that a preacher need be afraid of being too brilliant. But if we are loyal to Christ and the Church, we shall

use our strength, not to win personal honour, but to
prevail upon men to receive the teaching of Christ,
to trust in His promises, and to keep His commandments. Always, indeed, the highest kind of work
implies the renunciation of all thought of personal
display. The artist who is anxious that you should
see how perfectly he can paint, instead of being
anxious to paint perfectly, is certain to spoil his
picture. He will annoy you by wasting his power
on the satin coverlet of a bed or on a velvet dress,
instead of using it to tell the story which he is professing to place on the canvas. The speaker who,
instead of trying to enlarge your knowledge, to
awaken your sympathy for suffering, or fire your indignation against injustice, is trying to show how well
he can speak, will be equally unsuccessful. He may,
perhaps, win the admiration of foolish, half-educated
people, but he will excite no real interest, will kindle
no passion, will produce no deep and enduring impression: men of sense will call him an impostor.
He will not be even heard patiently by an audience
of any kind that is really in earnest about the subjects
he is professing to discuss. Ornamental speaking—
speaking which is nothing more than an exhibition of
intellectual strength, dexterity, and grace—may be
well enough on ceremonial occasions, at public dinners
and the like; but when the minds of men are occupied with grave questions, speaking of that sort is
hissed and howled down by a rough popular meeting,
and is got rid of in an equally summary manner by

the most cultivated and dignified assembly. If the affairs of a railway are going wrong, and the shareholders are afraid of losing not only their dividends but their capital, they want a man who can tell them facts on which they can rely, and who can show them a way out of their difficulties. The most witty and amusing speaker, the most ingenious, the most brilliant, will not be listened to unless he can make the position of affairs clearer, and unless he has some idea about how the property of the company can be kept together. If he is speaking only to show how well he can speak, the excited shareholders will either compel him to stop, or will throw him out of the window. In great national troubles, politicians do not want glittering periods, clever repartees, dainty epigrams : they want to be told how the famishing are to be fed, how crime is to be put down, how the discontent which menaces the stability of the national institutions is to be allayed, by what means war can be honourably averted, or by what means the nation can secure an honourable peace. A great statesman may also be a great orator. He may speak on these terrible questions, not only with terrible earnestness, but with incomparable brilliance, energy, and fire. His eloquence will in that case be of immense service to the principles and the policy which he is urging on the acceptance of the country. But if at such a time he is simply airing his rhetoric ; if he is as anxious to say graceful and humorous and beautiful things when he is dealing with dangers which threaten the lives and fortunes of the people and the honour and security of the state, as when he is proposing the toast of "The Ladies" at a lord mayor's banquet, he will provoke indignation and fierce contempt.

It is not possible—it is not desirable—that you should always preach under the strain of that agony of earnestness with which I trust you will be sometimes inspired. There are hours when the true minister of Christ is conscious that the celestial splendours are shining and glowing around him; and there are hours when every fibre of his nature shivers with terror at the prospect of the indignation and wrath, tribulation and anguish, which menace the finally impenitent. Such hours, I trust, will come to you. When they come, you will preach as if the fate of every irreligious man in your congregation were to be determined at once—determined by a single sermon—determined by the vehemence with which you denounce sin; the tenderness with which you speak of the infinite mercy of God; the fidelity with which you reaffirm the certain destruction of all who persist in their revolt against God's authority; the rapturous confidence with which you dilate on the glory, honour, and immortality which are the inheritance of all who trust in Christ and keep His commandments.

But though these great and critical times can come to us only occasionally—our strength would be consumed if they came often—every sermon that we preach should have a relation more or less direct to the rescue of the world from sin and its restoration to God.

To accomplish this end we ought to use in the work of the ministry all the resources that God has given us—our keenest and most vigorous intellectual powers, and whatever we have learnt from the speculations of philosophers and theologians, from the songs of poets, from the adventures of travellers, from the history of nations, from the discoveries of science, from grand and beautiful scenery, from great pictures, from glorious music, from the ruined monuments of ancient empires, from the triumphs of modern civilisation, from the achievements and sufferings of heroes and saints, and from the common lives of common men. We should spend time and strength in the endeavour to make all that we have to say as clear, as strong, as effective as we can make it; but if we have any sense of the tremendous issues of the conflict in which we are engaged between righteousness and sin, the love of God and the miseries of the human race, it will seem to us the greatest impiety to yield to the impulses of personal ambition, and we shall care for nothing except the glory of Christ and the salvation of mankind.

LECTURE III.

READING.

GENTLEMEN,—It is very possible that you may have thought me hard and uncharitable when I said in the last lecture that some men fail as preachers through intellectual indolence. Or perhaps you may have been generous enough to suppose that it was my ignorance of the religious life of America which led me to imagine that an American minister could ever be guilty of this vice.

But the position of a minister on this side of the Atlantic, as well as on the other, is obviously very likely to encourage desultory intellectual habits; and desultoriness and indolence are very near akin. With you, as with us, the judge has to be on the bench, the barrister in court, the solicitor at his office, the manufacturer at his works, the merchant at his desk, the tradesman at his counter, at a definite hour every morning; and not till a definite hour in the afternoon are they released. An indolent lawyer or man of business may, no doubt, go to his office, manufactory, or shop, half-an-hour or an hour late, and may often keep away altogether; while he is there he may waste his time over the newspaper, or in gossip with men that call in and are as indolent as himself; but the regular hours are a great help to regular habits; they form a kind of frame, which a man knows he has to fill up with work. With you, as with us, the minister is under no such external constraint. If the judge is not on the bench when the court opens, he hears of it from the newspapers the next morning; if the barrister is not ready to speak when the trial comes on, he has to meet the wrath of a furious client; but the minister may get up late, or he may spend half-an-hour extra over his breakfast, reading an interesting letter from the Paris correspondent in the *Times* or the *Tribune*, or an exciting debate in Parliament or in Congress, and may go into his study at half-past nine instead of nine without incurring any immediate penalty.

If a merchant leaves his letters unopened till the mail goes out, he knows that there is a chance of his receiving a sharp rebuke for not acknowledging a cheque, or he may miss a large order through not giving an immediate answer to an inquiry. But a minister, when he goes into his study on Tuesday or Wednesday morning, is under no compulsion to sit down to any definite occupation. He may be reading Dr. Dorner's "History of Protestant Theology," and has got half through the first volume; or he may have been working at the Epistle to the Romans, and has just reached the passage which has always perplexed him in the middle of the ninth chapter; but he looks up at his shelves, and his eye is caught by a novel of Hawthorne's or of Thackeray's ; or the postman brings the *New York Independent* or the *Spectator;* or he has just received the last book about Russia from the circulating library ; and so, for an hour or two, he reads the novel or the newspaper or the traveller's story, and before he turns to Dorner or to St. Paul the morning has half gone.

A minister is in danger of being betrayed into idle habits by a thousand temptations of which other men know nothing. He has not slept well, or he is suffering from a slight attack of indigestion ; the morning is fine ; there is nothing that absolutely compels him to keep at his desk, and he feels quite at liberty to stroll into the country. Or the weather is dull, and he is not in the mood for work ; there is no particular reason why he should not spend an hour in the newsroom ; or he persuades himself that he will be fulfilling a pastoral duty if he calls on the pleasantest family in his congregation, and so he idles away a couple of hours in gossip. He has been trying to make out the exact meaning of a text, and the longer he tries the more perplexed he becomes ; and when his perplexity is at the very worst, a lady calls to talk to him about a girl in her class in the Sunday-school, and when she goes he finds that it is only three-quarters of an hour to dinner time. He thinks it is of no use returning to the text, and so he amuses himself with the most amusing article in the magazine which happens to be on the table. When he was at college he had fixed hours for work, and wrote his letters when he could. Now that he is in the ministry, if he gets a letter from an old college chum by the morning post, and if he is not obliged to give the morning to one of his sermons for next Sunday, he thinks he may as well answer it at once, and so he consumes in letter-writing one of the prime hours of the day. Gentlemen, it is four and twenty years since I left college, and the temptations to desultoriness which I have either yielded to or mastered would enable me to go on for four and twenty hours with the story of the perils which will beset you as soon as you leave these walls. You will be ruined, your own hopes and the hopes of your friends will all be blighted, unless you resolve, with God's help, to stand firm and to work as hard when you become a minister as you have worked while at the university.

As to the subjects at which you should work, there is one piece of advice which I can give you with perfect confidence: it is one of those "commonplaces" to which I attach so much value, that I thought it worth while to cross the Atlantic to insist upon them: Keep up the knowledge which you have acquired at the university—your mathematics and science, if you can; your ancient and modern languages, whether you can or not. There are few things more mortifying than for a man who, when he was four and twenty, could read his Cicero and Tacitus, his Æschylus and Plato, freely, to be obliged to puzzle over them with a grammar and dictionary when he is forty-five; and to discover a few years later that to him the music of the ancient poets is silent, and that the ancient orators are dumb. That you will keep up, more or less perfectly, your New Testament Greek is a matter of course; but if I may judge from my own observation and from my own experience—I acknowledge it with shame—nothing is easier than for a minister to lose in a very few years his familiarity with Hebrew and Syriac. The precious results of months of hard work may vanish with extraordinary rapidity, and it will be very difficult to recover them. Of course, if a minister has once learnt to read his Hebrew Bible with ease and with keen interest, he will be certain to consult it often enough to prevent his knowledge of Hebrew from perishing altogether; and a knowledge of the genius of the language, which is invaluable in the study of the Old Testament, can never be lost when it is once acquired But we ought to read the Hebrew Text regularly, and if the habit is continued for only a few years after entering the ministry, our knowledge, instead of being lost, will soon be extended, and will be ours for life Syriac, although of immense use in New Testament exegesis, will vanish altogether unless you make a definite effort to retain it.

About German and French it is hardly necessary to speak. If you read these languages with ease before you leave the university, you will have such constant occasion to use them both, and you will find it so pleasant to enlarge your acquaintance with French and German literature, that you will be in no danger of forgetting what you have learnt.

But, as Schopenhauer said, "All that a man learns at the university is what he has to learn afterwards." There are some men, indeed, with a certain activity and superficial brilliance of intellect, who when they leave the university seem utterly unconscious of how much remains to be learnt. The theological creed of the Church to which they belong satisfies them perfectly; they have no suspicion that it does not contain a complete account of the whole mystery of God's relations to the human race. They remind one, in their cleverness as well as in their shallowness, of George Eliot's description of Gwendolen in "Daniel Deronda." "In the schoolroom her quick mind had taken readily that strong starch of unexplained rules and unconnected facts which saves ignorance from any painful sense of ignorance." But in the case of men whose intellectual life has any depth and freedom, and who want to know how the great facts of the universe really stand, Schopenhauer's words are broadly true—they have learnt very little more than how much they have to learn afterwards.

If I ventured to give you any very elaborate advice about the course of reading it will be expedient for you to follow when you are in the ministry, I should be guilty of unpardonable presumption. I have lived far too active a life to have any pretensions to speak with authority on that subject. About the books you should read, you will do well to obtain the judgment of your professors. But there are some general suggestions arising out of my own experience which may be of some use to you.

I assume that while you are here you will get a general view of the scheme of orthodox evangelical theology. You will carry away in your mind what may be called an index map of the whole territory of ascertained theological truth, as that territory is laid down by evangelical theologians of recognised authority. You will have learnt how they define the principal doctrines of their creed, the relations which they conceive to exist between these doctrines, and the general nature of the evidence by which it is supposed that the truth of the doctrines is demonstrated. If when you are beginning to preach you discover that here and there the lines of the map are beginning to fade, that perhaps great breadths of country have vanished altogether, so that you can give no account of them, I think you will do wisely to recover your knowledge as soon as you are able. Whether you accept the whole scheme or not, you ought to be in complete possession of it.

There are some preachers whose sermons—whatever they are preaching about—remind one of the conversation of people that have never been outside the village or the county in which they were born; people who would settle the affairs of a great nation in the interests of their own particular parish, and with no other knowledge than that which they have acquired in discussing and managing their own parochial business. Have you never listened to preachers of that sort—to men whose whole mind is occupied with a solitary doctrine or a solitary group of doctrines, and who seem to have no thought of the relations which these doctrines sustain to other truths, in which other men have the keenest interest, and which, when considered in the light of the history of the Church, are of the gravest importance? The odd thing is that these preachers, who in religious thought are the victims of a temper analogous to that narrow provincialism which, according to Mr. Matthew Arnold, is one of the chief infirmities or vices of the English nation, often claim to be " broad theologians." Their interest is narrowed to a very few great truths, and yet they imagine that their theology has the merit of exceptional breadth. You may do something towards protecting yourself against doctrinal provincialism by maintaining an intellectual acquaintance with truths in which you may be unable for a time to feel any deep moral or spiritual interest.

Your chief work, however, and your most fruitful work during the earlier years of your ministry, will probably consist in the investigation of great truths on which you have arrived at no satisfactory conclusion while at the university, or which you feel to be of such transcendent importance in relation to your personal religious life or to your ministerial work, that you are morally obliged to re-examine them with exceptional thoroughness and care. " Reading without purpose," says Lord Lytton, " is sauntering, not exercise. More is got from one book, on which the thought settles for a definite end in knowledge, than from libraries skimmed over by a wandering eye." [1]

[1] " Caxtoniana," vol. ii. p. 327.

The brilliant professor of Greek in the University of Edinburgh has said much the same thing in another form. "Reading, in the case of mere miscellaneous readers, is like the racing of some little dog about the moor, snuffing everything and catching nothing; but a reader of the right sort finds his prototype in Jacob, who wrestled with an angel all night, and counted himself the better for the bout, though the sinew of his thigh shrank in consequence."[1] If there is no great theological doctrine which you are compelled to reconstruct for yourself from its very foundations—none which you are obliged to re-examine in order to satisfy restless and clamorous fears that the walls are perhaps giving way or that the roof is unsound—I advise you to select some important doctrinal controversy, and to resolve to study it thoroughly. But the intenser your moral and religious interest is in the truth you are investigating, the more profitable, even intellectually, is your work likely to be.

In studying a doctrine, it is well to begin with its history. Learn how it grew; who invented the technical terms in which it is commonly defined; what heresies stimulated orthodox theologians to develop the truth more fully, and compelled them to define it more rigorously. Take particular notice of the religious mood of the age in which it was developed most rapidly and excited the most general and active controversy. Consider, too, what was the character of the dominant philosophy at successive periods in

[1] John Stuart Blackie "On Self Culture," p. 29.

the history of the controversy. Fix in your memory the men and the books that had chiefly to do with impressing on the doctrine the various changes of form through which it has passed. You may learn most of these facts from a general history of Dogma; if you can get a good special history of the particular doctrine which you are investigating, you will of course prefer it.

Then you will read for yourself a few of the great books, the names of which you have become familiar with in reading the history. You will soon learn how much of a book it is necessary to read for your purpose. In some cases you will be very likely to go wrong unless you read a book through, and read it through very carefully. In other cases, three or four chapters, or even a single chapter, will be enough. You must always try to be accurate in *placing* your author. If you do not remember the precise position of the controversy when he wrote, the errors which he regarded as most formidable, his conception of other doctrines more or less closely related to the doctrine under discussion, and the general spirit and modes of thought characteristic of his time, you will have no satisfactory understanding of his meaning. Athanasius wrote for the theologians of Alexandria, Antioch, Constantinople, and Rome, in the fourth century—not for Americans who were to live at New Haven, or for Englishmen who were to live in London or Birmingham, fifteen centuries after he was dead.

To retain the results of your reading, most of you, I

think, will find it necessary to read with your pen in your hand, and with a few sheets of paper on your desk. A brief analysis of the principal lines of thought in a great book, and occasional extracts containing the most formal definitions of the author's theory and his characteristic technicalities, will enable you to recall the whole substance of volumes which might otherwise fade altogether from your memory; unless, indeed, your memory is far less treacherous than my own. In preparing, two or three years ago, a series of lectures on the Atonement, I was able to save myself a large amount of labour by using notes of this kind which I had written sixteen or seventeen years before. If as you read you discuss in your notes the author's arguments and criticise his theories, you will obtain at the time a more complete mastery of his position, and your notes will be more useful to you afterwards.

The objections to this practice are obvious. The process of summarising what we are reading may become as purely automatic as the process of reporting what we are listening to. There is good reason to hope that the gentlemen of the press, to whose courtesy, intelligence, and skill all public men owe so much, are not cursed with any long remembrance of the speeches which they report with such surprising accuracy. Even when in their generous consideration and kindly compassion they correct our grammar for us, effect a rapid reconciliation between our nominatives and our verbs, achieve a surgical miracle on a sentence which broke its back as it leapt from our lips, I imagine that the intellectual operations by which all this is accomplished are almost mechanical. A writer in a recent number of the *Contemporary Review*, who says that he has had large experience of work of this kind, tells us that he has never found himself exhausted by working week after week for eighteen hours a day. "The reason," he says, "is, mainly, that in such work as in that of ordinary business the mind gets all the enormous help derivable from the laws of association. Link follows link, and the process goes upon an inclined plane to its goal."[1] Nature is sometimes kindly if she is often severe. When I think of the intellectual ability and varied accomplishments of many of the gentlemen who sit at the reporters' desk, and of the intolerable dulness and folly of many of the speeches which they have to transfer to their note-books, it is a consolation to be assured that the ear may listen and that the hand may write without the memory being charged with a solitary sentence. The sum of human misery is less than it seems.

But, gentlemen, your own note-books may be filled very much in the same way. The hand may work with the eye, as it may work with the ear, without any vigorous concurrence of the intellect, and what is read accurately and written accurately may be forgotten as soon as the note-book is closed. That you have to condense what you read, and make an abstract of it, does not secure you against this peril. Perhaps,

[1] *Contemporary Review*, April, 1877, p. 946.

instead of reading with your pen in your hand, as I have suggested, you may find it some protection if your permanent notes—the notes you intend to keep by you for reference—are made from memory, after you have mastered your author's meaning, and when the book has been returned to the shelves.

Notes of another kind and for another purpose may be made while you read. You may occasionally find it necessary to make a " scheme " of an argument in order to grasp it ; and you may often find it expedient to write out an argument in your own words and at some length in order to be sure that you understand it. In any case, while you are reading, be sure to keep your mind active. The habit into which I believe some students fall of making notes in the mechanical manner I have described, and " getting up " an author from their own dry abstract, deprives them of the generous stimulus and excitement which they would receive from direct contact with the vigorous activity of a powerful mind.

This dissertation on the advantages and perils of notes—you will take it for what it is worth—has led me away from the subject which suggested it—the manner in which you should read the great books which have contributed to the formation of the particular theological doctrine which you happen to be investigating.

To offer you any advice that is likely to be serviceable about the manner in which you read the Old and the New Testaments, in order to discover what authority the doctrine—either in the substance of it or in any of the forms which it has assumed—derives from the teaching of the apostles, and from the history and the discourses of our Lord Jesus Christ Himself, is a more difficult task. Two methods are open to you. If you adopt one of these you will find a great part of the necessary work done for you already. In books easily accessible, dogmatic and controversial theologians have arranged and discussed all the "proof-texts" that can be alleged in support of almost every conceivable doctrinal proposition. Calvinists of every shade, Arminians of every school, Romanists and Protestants, the representatives and advocates of conflicting or complementary theories on Original Sin, the Divine Decrees, the Moral Freedom of Man, the Person of Christ, the Atonement, the Nature and Effects of the New Birth, the Blessings included in Justification, the Conditions and Limits of Christian Perfection, the Sacraments, the Future of the Impenitent, have put in evidence every sentence and every phrase and every isolated word of Holy Scripture that could be supposed to give any support to their respective positions. Whatever question we may be investigating, the whole of the Scripture proof, so far as it is contained in "proof-texts," is already in our hands. The arguments and replies on the case may go on for centuries longer, as they have gone on for centuries already; but the inspired witnesses have been examined and cross-examined, their evidence is before the court, it seems unlikely that any further testimony can be obtained from them. If the sentence is to be determined by the authority of the witnesses, why need we examine them again? Why should we not be satisfied with considering their evidence as it has been illustrated by the ablest men who have had the conduct of the case on both sides?

I suppose that this is the common method of investigating the scriptural authority of a doctrine. I do not disparage it. The conclusiveness of the "proof-texts" which are usually adduced in behalf of the great doctrines of the evangelical creed appears to me decisive. It would be a sign of intellectual presumption and excessive self-confidence if we did not avail ourselves of the kind of evidence in support of a theory or against it which is ready to our hand. But I always feel that the least part of the Scripture proof of a great doctrine is that which appears in a catena of proof-texts; and I therefore recommend you not to suppose that you have all the light which the New Testament throws on any question which you are investigating, until, with that definite question before your mind, you have read the New Testament through from end to end.

I speak of the New Testament alone, partly because the New Testament may be read through in a very moderate amount of time, and partly because, in the determination of any theological inquiry of the kind to which I am now referring, the New Testament is practically decisive. Historically, the investigation of the religious ideas of the earlier books is profoundly interesting, and the roots and germs of Christian thought are to be found in the writings of Moses and the prophets. It must also be conceded that there are parts of the teaching of the New Testament which can hardly be accurately understood without an acquaintance with the ancient institutions and traditional hopes of the Jewish race. But practically the student of Christian doctrine is governed by the authority of the Christian Scriptures; and to ask you, whenever you are trying to arrive at a satisfactory conclusion on any doctrinal question, to read through the Old Testament as well as the New, would be to impose on you an intolerable burden.

As you read, you will come across the "proof-texts" which you have already considered in theological manuals and in controversial and dogmatic treatises. If I am not greatly mistaken, however, these texts will have new life and colour in them. You will come across them in their organic connection with the living system of thought to which they naturally belong. The words of Christ and of the apostles will receive an unexpected illustration from the circumstances which suggested them, from the emotion with which they were uttered, from the impression they produced on the people that heard them. A sentence may no doubt be perfectly intelligible when it is separated from the line of thought in which it occurs. The meaning of its terms may be fixed by the grammar and the lexicon beyond all reasonable controversy. But very often there can be no controversy at all if you read it as it stands; its meaning is determined without appeal by the movement of thought which precedes it and the movement of thought which follows it. The only true point of view from which to look at any sentence is the point to which the author has brought you by the path which leads up to it. Look at it from any other point, and you will not see it as he saw it, and as he intended that it should be seen by his readers.

Take, for instance, the words of St. Paul in Rom. v. 10: "For if, when we were enemies, we were reconciled to God by the death of his Son, much more, being reconciled, we shall be saved by his life." The passage is quoted in support of the doctrine that the death of our Lord Jesus Christ is the objective ground on which God receives into His favour those whom He had regarded with hostility on account of their sins. But this application is denied. It is contended that St. Paul meant that through the revelation of the infinite love of God in the death of Christ the hearts of those who regarded God with hostility are subdued to penitence, and that their hostility ceases. That the death of Christ has this effect is earnestly maintained by theologians who contend for an objective Atonement; but how are we to discover whether St. Paul was thinking of the moral influence exerted by our Lord's death on the hearts of men, or of its direct relations to God Himself as the ground on which He forgives sin? The lexicon does not help us. The noun translated "enemies" may mean either *those who are hostile to us* or *those to whom we are hostile*. The verb translated "we were reconciled" may mean either that *we have ceased to have any anger against some one else*, or that *some one else has ceased to have any anger against us*. The sentence standing alone may therefore bear alternative interpretations. It may mean that through the death of Christ we Christian people have ceased to be hostile to God—a truth upon which all Christian theologians are agreed; or that through the death of Christ the Divine wrath, which would have overtaken us sooner or later on account of our sin, is averted—a proposition which those who reject the doctrine of an objective Atonement deny. The passage is claimed with equal vehemence and equal confidence by two rival doctrines. The lexicon, as I have said, leaves the contest undecided. How is it to be determined?

How? Precisely in the same way in which we determine the meaning of a sentence which happens to catch our eye in the middle of a letter from a friend, when we are taking it out of the envelope. The sentence appears ambiguous at first sight, and if we looked at it alone, we might remain doubtful about its meaning for a month. But if we begin the letter and read it through, the ambiguity vanishes; and the sentence would never have seemed ambiguous at all if we had not happened to see it before we had read the earlier part of the letter.

And so, if your mind is filled and excited with the thoughts which occupy the first four chapters of the

Epistle to the Romans, it seems to me that you will be incapable of placing on this sentence in the fifth chapter any other interpretation than that which is imposed upon it by the theologians who contend for an objective Atonement. In the middle of the first chapter St. Paul dismisses the introductory matter with the noble words: "I am not ashamed of the gospel of Christ: for it is the power of God unto salvation to every one that believeth; to the Jew first, and also to the Greek." He then opens the doctrinal argument of the epistle by describing the gospel as a revelation of the righteousness of God. "Therein is the righteousness of God revealed from faith to faith; as it is written, The just shall live by faith"—or "The just by faith shall live." But he passes immediately to another revelation of a very different and most awful kind—the revelation of the wrath of God from heaven against all unrighteousness. In what a terrible way this wrath has been revealed in the heathen world, he tells us in the last half of the first chapter. To St. Paul, the moral corruption of the heathen was the sign that God, in His hot anger against their idolatry, had "given them up to uncleanness" and "unto vile affections." "As they did not like to retain God in their knowledge"—or, as it has been felicitously translated—"because they reprobated the knowledge of God, God gave *them* over to a reprobate mind." The crimes of which they were guilty—so St. Paul believed—were so foul, so gross, so revolting, that men would never have committed

them had not God, in His just resentment at their
revolt against His own authority, left them to themselves, and suffered them to be swept on from sin to
sin, from crime to ·crime, from shame to shame,
by the dark and turbid stream of their own worst
passions. The second chapter is a warning to the
Jews that their knowledge of the law, and the condemnation which they were so swift to pronounce on the
crimes of the Gentiles, would be no protection for
themselves against the judgment of God. God had
shown them wonderful goodness; but they might
despise the riches of His goodness and forbearance
and long-suffering, not seeing that the intention of the
Divine long-suffering was to lead them to repentance.
If, while they condemned others for breaking God's
law, they broke it themselves, then St. Paul declares
that in the hardness and impenitence of their hearts
they were treasuring up unto themselves wrath against
the day of wrath, and revelation of the righteous
judgment of God, "who will render to every man
according to his deeds: to them who by patient
continuance in well-doing seek for glory, honour,
and immortality, eternal life; but unto them that are
contentious, and do not obey the truth, but obey
unrighteousness, indignation and wrath, tribulation
and anguish, upon every soul of man that doeth evil,
of the Jew *first*, and also of the Gentile:" this is the
awful pre-eminence which St. Paul concedes to the
Jews who have the law and break it. It is an
appalling chapter. It is hot with the Divine wrath

against sin. While reading it I seem to be breathing the burning air which rises from streams of fiery lava, and my feet are scorched with the ashes which have just been thrown from the furnace of a volcano.

In the early part of the third chapter the last hopes of the Jews are swept away. If they supposed that, although they were sinners, they would escape the Divine wrath, becáuse " to them were committed the oracles of God "—and this was their chief distinction —let them turn to those very oracles. Do the Jewish Scriptures speak gently of the sins of Jews? In times of national corruption did psalmists and prophets shrink from uttering fierce words of condemnation? You remember the chain of passages which St. Paul quotes from the ancient Jewish books—passages which express anger and hatred against Jewish sins. " Their throat is an open sepulchre ; with their tongues they have used deceit ; the poison of asps is under their lips ; their mouth. is full of cursing and bitterness ; their feet are swift to shed blood ; destruction and misery are in their ways, and the way of peace have they not known ; there is no fear of God before their eyes." To be a Jew is not enough to shelter a man from the Divine wrath. What things soever the law saith, it saith to them who are under the law ; and the very end for which these words were written was that every mouth might be stopped—the mouth of the Jew as well as of the Gentile—and that so the whole world might become conscious of its guilt before God. " By the deeds of the law shall no flesh be justified in God's sight, for by the law is the knowledge of sin."

It is from the Divine wrath that the world needs deliverance, and the deliverance is accomplished through Him whom God hath set forth for Himself as a Propitiation—through faith—has set forth as a Propitiation in His blood; to declare His righteousness, that He might be just and the Justifier of him that believeth in Jesus. A Propitiation turns wrath aside.

The fourth chapter is a parenthesis, and is intended to show, by an appeal to two of the greatest names in Jewish history—Abraham and David—that this doctrine of justification by faith instead of by the works of the law was not new. In the fifth chapter, St. Paul exults in the blessings which come to us from the revelation of the Divine righteousness in Christ. Read the chapter in the fierce light of all that has been said in the earlier part of the epistle, and you will be incapable of missing its meaning. We were in peril of the wrath of God, but, "being justified by faith, we have peace with God through our Lord Jesus Christ;" that is, God is at peace with us. "By Christ we have also access into the grace wherein we stand." We who were exposed to the Divine anger are now standing in the Divine favour; and more than this, we who had reason to dread the revelation of the righteous judgment of God—the indignation and wrath, the tribulation and anguish, which have been threatened against every soul of man that doeth evil—even we "triumph in the hope of the glory of God." Link after link is added to the golden chain, till the apostle exclaims, "God establishes—makes certain—his love toward us, in that while we were yet sinners Christ died for us; much more then, being now justified by his blood, we shall be saved from the WRATH through him." The wrath which still threatens the impenitent and unbelieving, St. Paul cannot forget; but through Christ we who believe shall be saved from it. "*For if when we were enemies*,"—when the wrath of God was impending over us on account of our sin,—"*we were reconciled to God*,"—received into His favour, into "the grace wherein we stand,"—"*by the death of his Son, much more being reconciled shall we be saved by his life*,"—saved in the awful hour when His wrath against sin will be revealed.

In this case a "proof-text" receives a definite and more intensely vivid meaning when we read it in its true place than when we read it in a classified list of quotations. There are other cases in which passages which could have no place in such a list may contribute materials of great value in relation to the doctrine we are investigating. We may sometimes discover, for example, what the apostles must have taught by observing the false impressions which their teaching produced upon their converts, impressions which are corrected in the epistles. St. Paul, in his preaching at Thessalonica, must have given great prominence to that glorious revelation of Christ which is the supreme hope of the Church, or it would have been impossible for the Thessalonians to imagine that their Christian brethren who had died had sustained an irreparable loss, and would not fully share the glory of those who will be " alive " at " the coming of the Lord."

The slanders of the enemies of the apostles are an indication of what the apostolic doctrine must have been. That it should have been possible for the enemies of St. Paul to charge him with teaching that men may "do evil that good may come," and " sin that grace may abound," throws an intense light on St. Paul's teaching about justification.

Further; we should never forget that in the apostolic epistles it is assumed that the persons to whom they are addressed are already acquainted with the elementary facts and truths of the Christian revelation. It is very rarely, therefore, that the apostles state in a categorical form that our Lord Jesus Christ was divine ; but that they believed in His divinity is shown in the reverence and boundless love with which they speak of Him, in their habitual recognition of His authority over their moral life, their fervent gratitude for what He had done and suffered for themselves and all mankind ; it is shown by the immense significance which they attach to His sufferings and death, and by their trust in His mercy for the forgiveness of sin, and in the power of His life for strength to do the will of God ; it is shown by the awe and the fear with which they anticipate the hour in which He will judge the world. They very rarely affirm in so many words that Christ died for our sins, or that it is necessary to be born again of the Holy Spirit in order to enter the Divine kingdom and to inherit eternal glory; but these truths are implied in all that they say about the great prerogatives and hopes of the Christian Church. One of the surest methods of ascertaining the contents of the apostolic faith is, therefore, to study closely the elements and characteristics of the apostolic life.

How these principles will affect your method of reading an epistle, in order to discover the relation of the writer to any particular theological doctrine on which you are trying to form a judgment, needs no elaborate illustration. You will not look merely for passages in which the doctrine is definitely asserted. You will ask whether the writer's supposed faith in the doctrine accounts for his way of conducting an argument—for what he omits that would naturally have occurred to him if he had held a hostile theory, as well as for what he has written; whether it is the natural and necessary complement of truths which he explicitly affirms; whether it is implied in his thanksgivings and prayers; whether it explains any of the precepts which the epistle contains and the motives by which they are enforced; whether if the doctrine had not been a recognised part of the Christian faith some of these precepts would have been necessary; or whether if the precepts had been necessary they would have been enforced by different motives; whether the errors which are corrected in the epistle — errors of opinion or errors of spirit and practice — could have originated in a natural misapprehension of the apostolic doctrine on the subject of your inquiry, and if so, in what form the doctrine must have been taught, to render the misapprehension possible.

These same general principles of investigation may be applied to the history and teaching of our Lord Jesus Christ contained in the Gospels. Suppose that He had been a man and nothing more—would not the story of His life, and those passages of it which are most truly human, have run differently, even though the story had been written by the most unintelligent and fanatical of His disciples, or by the most unintelligent and fanatical of their converts? Suppose that He had come—not to die for the sins of men, and to assert His own claims to supreme moral authority over the human race, but simply to teach nobler ethics and a nobler religious faith than the world had learnt before—would even His ethical teaching have assumed its present shape, would his religious teaching have been given in its present tone? The Sermon on the Mount — is there nothing in the manner of it which implies that He claimed to be more than a prophet? The story of His relations to Mary His mother—is there nothing in it which suggests that He was infinitely more than her Son? The facts which illustrate His relations to His human friends—do they not provoke many inquiries which receive no satisfactory solution except from the theory which attributes to Him a superhuman dignity and glory? How was it that He took it for granted that it was their highest moral and religious duty to forsake all in order to serve Him? How was it that He never consulted them? How was it that though on more than one occasion He prayed in their presence, He never prayed with them? How was it that He never consoled them in their moral weakness by assuring them that He too was conscious of the weakness which is common to humanity? How was it that He never confessed sin?[1]

The results of this method of investigating the scriptural evidence in favour of any theological doctrine may not always be easily available for controversial purposes; they may sometimes be too subtle for use in your sermons; but, if I may judge from my own experience, they will give great strength and certainty to your own theological convictions, and will continually suggest lines of thought which will make your preaching fresh, vigorous, and instructive.

I hoped that I should have been able to finish this afternoon all the suggestions I intended to offer you about ministerial reading, but I find that I have some things to say which must be reserved for the next lecture.

[1] See the argument of this paragraph elaborated in Harvey Goodwin's Hulsean Lectures for 1846, "The Glory of the only-begotten of the Father seen in the Manhood of Christ."

LECTURE IV.

READING (CONCLUDED).

GENTLEMEN,—It is hardly necessary to remind you that a man may have clear and strong theological convictions ; may have a large acquaintance with the contents of the Holy Scriptures and with the history of the doctrinal thought of the Church, and may yet be a dull and ineffective preacher. There are many men whose knowledge is rich and varied, but who cannot teach. And of those who can teach —that is, address a solitary faculty of human nature, the understanding—how few there are who can compel every province in the broad continent of the intellectual and moral life of man to confess their authority and power. It is one thing to have a clear perception of Christian truth ourselves ; it is quite another thing to be able to make the truth clear to the common mind ; to force the conscience to feel its pressure ; to disturb the slumbers of those mysterious instincts which vindicate our kinship to God ; to call to the aid of the Gospel all the friendly powers of man's moral life ; to speak of the divine anger so as to rouse the fears of men ; to kindle their imagination by illustrations of the nobleness, and beauty, and blessedness of a life in God ; to move them to penitence, and to inspire them with faith in the infinite love of the Lord Jesus Christ.

You, gentlemen, are to be preachers. The instrument you have to master stands before you — the soul of man. You have to learn how to handle every stop and to touch every key, and to bring out of it the sweetest, richest, saddest, wildest, most stately and most triumphant spiritual music. I know that you can do nothing except though the concurrence of the great power of God ; but if I understand anything of the laws which determine the success of our preaching, we have no right to hope that God will work with us unless we work ourselves. No matter how earnestly we pray, we may take it for granted that God will not do His part unless we do ours. "Work without prayer," said an old English writer, whose name I have forgotten, " is atheism ; and prayer without work is presumption." If we have to work at all we should try to work in the most effective way.

There is a saying of St. Paul's which is often quoted inaccurately, and the false quotation produces a most pernicious impression. He is represented as saying, "Paul may plant and Apollos may water, but God must give the increase." However true this may be—and I do not for a moment dispute its truth—the quotation in that form seems to imply that between human work and the divine blessing, which alone can make it successful, there is only a casual and uncertain relation. I prefer to take St. Paul's words as he wrote them : — " I planted, Apollos watered, but God gave the increase." St. Paul did not mean to imply that after we have done our best it is as likely as not that God may do nothing. The Corinthian Christians were divided into factions. They quarrelled about the merits and claims of their religious teachers. St. Paul reminds them that whoever may do the work, the glory of its success belongs to God.

The inference which is sometimes drawn from these words, even when they are not misquoted, is as preposterous as it is mischievous. Since the success of our work comes from God, it is argued that knowledge — though as profound as St. Paul's — and eloquence—though as fervent as the eloquence of Apollos—count for nothing. It would be equally reasonable to argue that because the vintage comes from God it counts for nothing whether or not the vine-grower understands his business and works hard in the vineyard. God gives no vintage if men plant elms instead of vines. The vine itself will bear no grapes unless God gives "the increase;" but it may be so planted that it will be certain to die in a week ; it may be so cultivated, or the cultivation may be so neglected, that the life and vigour of the vine will be fatally injured.

Knowledge is clearly of some importance. A man must know something about Christian truth or he cannot preach the gospel at all. And who can tell when he knows so much that more knowledge will be useless to him ? We are surely trusting just as much in the "arm of flesh" when we insist that a minister must know a little as when we insist that it is desirable that he should know a great deal.

"Yes," it may be replied, "we admit that the more a minister knows about God the better he is qualified for his work, but what we object to is a solicitude about style and rhetoric and human learning; this shows that ministers are relying on the wisdom of men and not on the power of God." And yet, I suppose that if the good people who talk to us in this way send a missionary to China to preach the Gospel, they expect him to learn Chinese. Why it should be supposed that a Christian missionary in China betrays no want of faith in God when he learns the words of the Chinese language from a dictionary, its construction from a grammar, its idioms from intercourse with the people, but that a Christian minister in the United States, or in England, is "trusting in an arm of flesh" when he tries to increase his knowledge of English by studying the great English authors, and when he listens to homiletical lectures and reads books on rhetoric, in order that he may learn how to speak more clearly and more effectively, is to me wholly incomprehensible. Since we have to preach, we ought to learn how to preach well.

Some men speak contemptuously of lectures on preaching and treatises on the science or art of rhetoric. For myself, I have read scores of books of this kind, and I have never read one without finding in it some useful suggestion. I advise you to read every book on preaching that you can buy or borrow, whether it is old or new, Catholic or Protestant, English, French, or German. Learn on what principles the great preachers of other churches as well as of your own, of other countries as well as of your own, of ancient as well as of modern times, have done their work. If your experience corresponds with mine, the dullest and most tedious writer on this subject will remind you of some fault that you are committing habitually, or of some element of power which you have failed to use.

But useful as you will find the study of the theory of preaching, you will probably find that the study of the sermons of successful preachers is equally useful. The artist is not satisfied with reading scientific treatises on Perspective and lectures on Painting, nor even with watching sea and land, mountain and glen, forest and river, under their changing aspects, from the cold grey light of the early morning to the fiery splendours of sunset; he spends months and years, if he is able, in the galleries of Florence and Rome, of France, Germany, and England, trying to learn how the immortal masters of form and colour worked the miracles in the presence of which generation after generation has stood with wonder and delight. You will derive great advantage from following their example.

Of Chrysostom and the other famous preachers of the ancient Church I will not venture to speak; but let me advise you to study the sermons of Bossuet, Bourdaloue, and Massillon, of Lacordaire and Ravignan, of

Monod and Bersier; of Latimer and Jeremy Taylor, Barrow, South, and Tillotson; of Howe and Owen and Watts; of Chalmers, Edward Irving, and Guthrie; of Robert Hall, and Dr. Maclaren of Manchester, and Charles Spurgeon; of Thomas Binney and James Parsons; of John Henry Newman and Dr. Pusey; of Archdeacon Manning—about the sermons of Cardinal Manning I know nothing; of Frederick Robertson and Canon Liddon. The merits of American preachers, both living and dead, are better known to you than they can be to me. From some of your living preachers I have learnt very much; so much that I have often felt how superfluous and even presumptuous it is for me to have crossed the Atlantic to deliver these lectures; among the dead I am under exceptional obligations to Jonathan Edwards and Mr. Finney. To these names I trust you will allow me to add that of another man, from whose theology I differ widely, but for whose power and resources as a preacher, and for whose courage in standing by the cause of freedom in evil times, I have the greatest admiration—I refer to the late Theodore Parker.

Of the German preachers I know too little to have the right to select the names of those who are best worth reading. Of the Italian preachers I know only one—Segneri, some of whose sermons were translated a few years ago by an English clergyman; they are very striking.

If you read sermons wisely, it will not be with the hope of discovering "suggestive thoughts," as we are accustomed to call them in England—thoughts which, with a very little cultivation, you may grow into sermons of your own ;—but you will read with a keen eye for the qualities which have given to the great preachers of our own and of past times the power they exerted over the men that listened to them. You will notice what subjects they preached on, and the sort of texts they selected. You will try to find out the principles and methods which governed them, consciously or unconsciously, in the arrangement and development of their principal thoughts. You will ask whether the introduction to the sermon you are reading really introduces what comes after it ; you will observe how the preacher effects his " transitions "—to which French preachers attach so much importance— from one principal division of his subject to another. You will endeavour to discover what is the secret of his success in investing very familiar truths with fresh interest. You will consider the amount and the kind of truth which he has been able to present to a congregation in a single discourse. You will notice how he handles his illustrations. You will especially study the methods in which he appeals, directly or indirectly, to the hopes and fears of men, to their moral imagination, to their conscience, to their sense of shame, to their susceptibility to gratitude, to all the active elements of their moral and religious nature.

In judging of sermons you will, of course, take into account the kind of effect which the men who preached them are known to have produced. The sermons which have been preached in great revivals deserve special study. If they did their work, you may take it for granted that there is much to be learnt from them. For the practical ends of your ministry you may find it far more profitable to study the sermons of the late Mr. Finney, and to listen to my friend Mr. Moody, than to spend your strength on the preachers that were admired by the Court of Louis XIV.

You ought to study the speeches of great secular orators in the same way. The speeches of Lord Erskine, of Charles James Fox, of Plunket, of Grattan, of Lord Brougham, of Mr. Bright, will repay careful reading. The varying merits of your own orators are known better to you than to me. In reading them you will not be satisfied with admiring "fine passages." The best and strongest parts of a speech — the parts which reveal the true genius of the orator — are not always the most brilliant. It was not with the decorated hilt of his sword that the old knight cleaved in two the skull of his enemy; nor was it the shining plume on his helmet that protected his own head. Very often the real strength of a speech lies in no particular passage which you can learn and declaim, but in the skilful arrangement of its arguments, illustrations, and appeals; and the keen edge of it is sometimes to be found in passages which are destitute of ornament, and which may even look almost careless in their style.

The way to make your study of a great speech really useful is to place yourself in the position of the

speaker ; to remember his previous history, the kind of
authority he had with his audience, the confidence or
the distrust, the enthusiasm or the hostility, with which
they regarded him. You must also recall the position
of the cause he was defending or attacking, the knowledge which his audience possessed of its merits and
demerits, the measure of their sympathy with the side
to which the speaker was committed, or of their antagonism to it. Try to understand what were the weak
points in his case and what were the strong points ;
what aspects of it were likely to secure the goodwill
of the audience, and what aspects of it were likely to
provoke hostile prejudice. Then look into the speech
and try to learn how all the conditions under which it
was delivered influenced the orator in the tone which
he assumed when he began to speak — made him
courteous or defiant, resolute and uncompromising, or
modest and conciliatory. If his tone changed as he
went along, ask why, and whether the change was wise.
Consider, too, how the conditions under which he was
speaking determined him to use some arguments
which may not strike you as being in themselves very
conclusive, and to avoid others which in themselves
may seem to you to have much greater force.
Consider how these conditions influenced him in the
arrangement of his topics, in his allusions and illustrations. Take particular notice of the way in which
he explains to his audience what he thinks they may
have misunderstood, and does it without implying that
they are ignorant, or that they have formed their

opinions hastily and rashly. Observe how he presents over and over again, in different forms, the strong parts of his argument, the facts, the inferences, with which he is most anxious to fill the minds of those whom he is trying to convince. Watch him in his methods of relieving the attention of his audience ; consider the use he makes of humour, or of wit, or of imagination. Observe how, by a passing allusion, he touches the deepest sympathies, or the just pride, or perhaps the ambition and the self-interest, of those whom he is addressing. " Fine passages " may occur here and there ; but a true orator never uses them for their own sake. He wants to convince his audience of the innocence of his client ; of the soundness of the political principles which he is defending, or the rottenness of the political principles which he is assailing ; of the merits of his own political friends and the demerits of his opponents. If " fine passages " will help him, well and good ; but if not, then he does without them.

The resources and methods of the preacher differ, no doubt, from the resources and methods of the legal or political orator ; but you may discover in the speeches of great lawyers, statesmen, and agitators, many suggestions which, if you are wise, you will be able to use in the preparation of your sermons. Reading of this kind will also do something to prevent that want of completeness and symmetry in your intellectual development which is likely to be the result of exclusive devotion to theological studies. Thomas Taylor, the Platonist, used to show with pride two of his fingers which, in copying out the manuscripts of Proclus and Plotinus in a fine Greek hand, had been so bent that he had lost the use of them. "It would be well," says Hazlitt, who tells the story, "if our deep studies often produced no other crookedness and deformity."[1]

To avoid this "crookedness and deformity," and to maintain free intellectual relations with cultivated men who are not professional theologians, as well as to satisfy your own intellectual tastes, which, I trust, you will always think it a duty to keep healthy and active, there are other kinds of reading which you will not permit yourselves to neglect. History—and especially the history of your own country; the lives of men who have exerted a great and critical influence on the fortunes of great nations, who have originated remarkable religious movements, or who are famous in literature and art; the leading and authoritative books on political economy; books which illustrate the laws of social and national life; books which present the ascertained results of the investigations of modern science: all these will enrich your thought, will prevent you from becoming mere sermon-makers and theological pedants.

It is hardly necessary that I should suggest that you should read the books which, through century after century, have succeeded in charming the imagination and the hearts of men living in different countries, and

[1] "Sketches and Essays," p. 6.

speaking different tongues. You may not be able to see the bazaars of Cairo, Damascus, and Bagdad, but from "The Arabian Nights" you may learn more about the East than some people seem to know when they come home after a long Eastern tour; and "Don Quixote" may teach you as much as a month in Spain. Other books, not as famous as these, have as strong a claim upon all who speak the English tongue. It is a disgrace for an American or an Englishman not to have read "Robinson Crusoe;" and, if I may dare to say it, Bunyan's "Pilgrim's Progress" and "Holy War" are quite as profitable reading for our purposes as very much that was written by Augustine himself.

Having found courage to say this, I think I may as well ruin myself altogether by saying something more. At the risk of bringing down upon myself the sharp and scornful condemnation of the more learned persons in my audience, I will venture to add that I do not recommend you to refuse to read books that have a merely ephemeral popularity. If you were all destined to occupy university chairs, I might offer you different advice—supposing that, in that case, I could presume to offer you any advice at all—and yet it may be possible that even in the library of a professor of ecclesiastical history, above the shelves on which the folios of the Magdeburg centuriators and the rival Annals of Baronius stand side by side in solemn and awful dignity, there may be a shelf that gives a kindly refuge to "Helen's Babies;" and I trust that I am guilty of no irreverence if I imagine that even a professor of dogmatic theology, if he has unfortunately forgotten to put a volume of Athanasius or Aquinas into his portmanteau to while away the tedious hours of a railway journey, may go to a book-stall and buy a volume of Mark Twain's, or the last book by Bret Harte. I am conscious, however, that in these wild speculations I am venturing on very thin ice. But we who are not professors have to interest and impress common people; and whatever may be said about the dissipation of intellectual energy incurred by the attempt to read all the books that other men are talking about, I am convinced that we ought to keep up a fair acquaintance with contemporary literature. If we know nothing of the books that our congregations are reading, they will soon learn to think of us as intellectual foreigners—strangers to their ways and thoughts, ignorant of a large part, and in some respects the most interesting part, of their lives.

You will not misunderstand me. Your strength must be given to grave and continuous studies. You will fence round the prime hours of the day and keep them for hard work, or else you will be lost. But the humblest cottage should have a flower-bed as well as a potato plot; and even in England, where ground is becoming scarce, I should be sorry to see the village green ploughed up and turned into a corn-field. This desultory and miscellaneous reading will give you a certain intellectual exhilaration, and will enable you to do your severer work with greater vigour.

I always envy the men who have an intellectual hobby—a hobby which they learned to ride when they were young—perhaps when they were boys; and on which, even in their busiest years, they continue to trot with as much enjoyment as ever. To have some pursuit in which we are keenly interested, lying outside our serious and imperative occupations, is a great intellectual refreshment. It does not very much matter what the pursuit is. Some men collect ancient coins and learn all about them; some men care for a particular department of natural science; some concentrate their historical reading on a particular century in the history of a particular country; some men devote themselves to a particular poet and to all the literature that illustrates what he has written; some to Egypt, some to Holland, some to Florence, some to Rome. If we do not give to these by-subjects the time and energy which we ought to give to the main business of life, they are an unqualified advantage to us.

Though we may have nothing that can be called a "hobby," we may have our favourite books. There is a wonderful charm in reading a book every line of which is familiar to you. It is like talking over school days and college days with an old friend. You have heard him tell every one of his tales a dozen times; you know as soon as he begins a story how it will end; you anticipate his look when he comes to his comic passages, and the tone in which he will tell them, and the precise point at which he will explode in irrepressible laughter ; but the old stories from the old friend have a greater charm than the fresh wit of a stranger. Or, it is like walking along the roads of a pleasant country in which for many years we have spent our holiday. We know the trees and the brooks and the bridges ; we look for the picturesque cottages which we shall have to pass ; we are prepared for the view of the distant mountains or the shining sea, which is caught at a particular turn in the road : in seeing the old objects one after another, when we have been away from them for a few months, there is a kind of pathetic surprise which touches us far more deeply than the surprise of novelty.[1]

If books are anything more to us than mere paper and printer's ink, if, while we read, to use the felicitous language of Bolingbroke, "we live with men who lived before us, and inhabit countries which we have never seen," we shall have our elect friends in our library as well as among living men and women ; and there will be books that will have the same kind of power over our imagination and our heart as the village among the hills which we dream about when we are worn down with our winter's work, and in which summer after summer we have found rest and health and vigour.

The old books remain while everything else passes away. The chances and changes of this mortal life do not touch them. The fields in which we picked

[1] See Note at the end of the Lecture.

wild flowers and played cricket when we were boys are covered with dreary streets. The houses in which we lived have been pulled down, and there are unfamiliar buildings on the site of our old homes. The churches in which we worshipped have been enlarged or rebuilt. The preachers to whom we listened are dead, and the faces we remember so well are no longer seen in the old pews ; or, if they are there still, they are greatly changed. The brilliant and romantic lads of our youth have become hard and prosy men ; the bright wild girls have become very uninteresting matrons ; the aged people, whose sorrows and loneliness we pitied, or whose sanctity we reverenced, have all passed away. We ourselves are conscious, as the years drift by, that our strength is not what it once was ; that there is less elasticity in our step ; that we are more easily tired ; that our sight is at times a little dim and our hearing a little dull. But we open our books, and the vanished years return. Time has run back and fetched the age of gold.[1] The fancy of Jeremy Taylor is as free and as fresh, and the wit of South is as keen, and the fervour of Baxter is as intense, as when we first heard them preach. Charles James Fox is still speaking with undiminished energy and fire on the Westminster scrutiny. We knew old Lear when we were boys ; he is no older now. Most of the young men and maidens

[1] " For if such holy song
Inwrap our fancy long,
Time will run back and fetch the age of gold."
Milton's " Hymn on the Nativity."

whose love passages entertained us when we ourselves were young are old married people, and occasionally wrangle over the expenses of housekeeping; but Romeo and Juliet are courting still:

"For ever he will love and she be fair." [1]

What books you will choose as your intimate friends will depend upon your humour and taste. Dr. Guthrie's choice seemed to me charming. He told me that he read through four books every year—the Bible, "The Pilgrim's Progress," four of Sir Walter Scott's novels, which he reckoned as one book, and a fourth book, which I have forgotten, but I think it was "Robinson Crusoe." You will choose some books because they soothe and quiet you; some because they are as invigorating as mountain air; some because they amuse you by the shrewdness of their humour; some because they give wings to your fancy; some because they kindle your imagination.

But there are books of another kind, which have graver claims. Every great and original writer has his characteristic intellectual method. He has his own way of approaching every question that he discusses; his own way of investigating the evidence of every doubtful proposition; his own way of analysing and destroying the arguments which are alleged in support of a position which he rejects; and his own way of developing the proof of a position which he maintains. If you read him carefully you will also

[1] "For ever wilt thou love and she be fair."—Keats's "Ode to a Grecian Urn."

discover that there are certain settled principles of judgment which are explicitly or implicitly recognised in all his intellectual decisions. These correspond to those great constitutional principles and those authoritative legal maxims which are current in the law courts and which govern an infinite variety of cases. It is another quality of a writer of original and creative genius that he is never satisfied with dead thought. Whether his ideas are true or false, they have such vital force in them that they are capable of indefinite growth, and are the roots of whole systems of speculation.

Close familiarity with a few great books will do more than anything else to enrich and discipline your mind. If we walk day after day with some illustrious writer, we shall naturally fall into his pace. Thinking his thoughts over and over again, we shall unconsciously adopt his methods of thinking. He will train us to his own habits of caution, moderation, and sagacity. He will inspire us with his own courage and boldness. We shall catch, without knowing it, and without any attempt at imitation, something of that intellectual manner which gives to everything that he has written an inimitable nobleness, or vigour, or grace. We shall become masters, not only of all the thoughts which are actually expressed in his books, but of very much that these thoughts imply. We shall fully develop truths which were present to him in a rudimentary form. We shall not be satisfied with coming into possession of the rich golden grain which he was able to garner, we shall drive our own plough across the fields which he first reclaimed from the waste; we shall practise his methods of cultivation; we shall sow the seed which he has left us; and we shall reap fresh harvests of our own.

Perhaps you may say that I am expecting from you an enormous amount of intellectual labour—an amount of intellectual labour which you may even fear would be inconsistent with the culture of your personal religious life and with hearty and unreserved devotion to your ministerial duties. In England, during the last thirty years, we have seen from time to time very unpleasant indications of a distrust of the influence of literature and learning on ministerial earnestness and efficiency. We are told that the Church does not need more intellectual culture in the ministry, but more spiritual fervour; that we spend too much time with our books and too little in active, energetic labour for the salvation of mankind. The good men who indulge in complaints of this kind are in the habit of uttering loud lamentations over the disappearance of the simpler piety and deeper devotion of our fathers. The traditions of Puritan faith and fervour are appealed to in order to shame and to stimulate our languid zeal. They cannot be invoked too often.

But what kind of men were these saintly ancestors of ours? Did the fire of their devotion burn so high because it was not choked with an excess of intellectual fuel? Were they better men than we are because they had less learning? Were they more zealous as ministers because they were less industrious as students?

John Howe was a great theologian and a great preacher; but he was something more. "None can peruse his writings," says his biographer, my own accomplished tutor, Mr. Henry Rogers, "without seeing in almost every page traces of his ardent admiration for Plato, and proofs that it was the admiration of a kindred mind."[1] But if the lofty idealism of Plato was most akin to his own genius, his "Living Temple" shows that he had an extraordinary mastery of the whole range of philosophical speculation. He knew the modern writers as well as the ancient. A considerable part of his greatest treatise is a reply to Spinoza; and he had studied Descartes, and speaks of him as "that great and justly admired master in this faculty," and "that famed restorer and improver of some principles of the ancient philosophy."[2] The theological learning of John Owen, in its immense extent and its massiveness, has sometimes reminded me of those vast ruins which still perpetuate the grandeur of ancient Rome. Some years ago, when I was young and had my own ambitions, I extracted a passage from Richard Baxter—I forget in which of his works it is to be found—in which he tells us in confidence the nature and variety of his own studies. He says: "I have looked over Hutten, Vives, Erasmus,

---

[1] "Life of Howe," p. 20.
[2] "Works," vol. iii. pp. 53, 75.

Scaliger, Salmasius, Casaubon, and many other critical grammarians, and all Gruter's critical volumes. I have read almost all the physic and metaphysics I could hear of. I have wasted much of my time among loads of historians, chronologers, and antiquaries. I despise none of their learning; all truth is useful. Mathematics, which I have least of, I find a pretty, manlike sport. . . . I have higher thoughts of the schoolmen than Erasmus and our other grammarians had: I much value the method and sobriety of Aquinas, the subtlety of Scotus and Ockham, the plainness of Durandus, the solidity of Ariminensis, the profundity of Bradwardine; the excellent acuteness of many of their followers; of Aureolus, Capreolus, of Bannes, Alvarez, Zumel, &c.; of Mayro, Lychetus, Trombeta, Faber, Meurisse, Rada, &c.; of Ruiz, Pennatus, Suarez, Vasquez, &c.; of Hurtado, of Albertinus, of Lud. à Dola, and many others."

Their studies did not lessen the ardour of their zeal. These were the men who were the ministers of our churches when religious faith was most robust and when religious earnestness was most intense. It was the teaching of men like these that gave muscle and fibre to the religious life of the founders of New England. Among the early ministers of your own churches were men of the same masculine and noble type. They were great students as well as great preachers, and their studies helped their preaching.

Some accounts have come down to us of the personal habits of the men of those times. John

Owen, during several years of his university life, allowed himself only four hours' sleep, but kept himself in health and vigour by those athletic exercises which enabled him, when he was Vice-Chancellor of Oxford, to seize with his own hands a refractory student and carry him off to prison, to the amazement of the gownsmen who were intending to effect a rescue. Edmund Calamy studied sixteen hours a day while chaplain to the Bishop of Ely, read Augustine through five times, and, among his other studies, mastered the immense literature which was created during the controversy between Bellarmine and his opponents. Matthew Poole, while preparing his "Synopsis," which occupied him ten years of his life, rose every morning between three and four o'clock, worked till eight or nine, when he ate a raw egg, worked on again till twelve o'clock, when his ascetic meal was repeated, and did not leave his desk till the afternoon was far advanced. In the evening we are told that he used to visit a friend and be very merry till supper, after which he turned the talk to grave and serious things, and then went home. Joseph Alleine, who died in Taunton Gaol, seems to have worked as hard as the rest. When he married, he received a letter of congratulation from an old college friend, who said that he had some thoughts of following his example, but wished to be wary, and would therefore take the freedom of asking him to describe the inconveniences of a married life. Alleine replied: "Thou wouldst know the inconveniences of a wife, and I will tell thee. First of all, whereas thou risest constantly at four in the morning, or before, she will keep thee till six ; secondly, whereas thou usest to study fourteen hours in the day, she will bring thee to eight or nine ; thirdly, whereas thou art wont to forbear one meal at least in the day for thy studies, she will bring thee to thy meat. If these are not mischief enough to affright thee, I know not what thou art." So that all the troubles of these studious men did not come from a persecuting Government. We might add a deeper pathos to the story of their sufferings and constancy by dilating with sympathetic eloquence on the sorrows which came on them from " those of their own households," from wives who deprived them of their liberty to study fourteen hours a day and cruelly robbed them of the joys of early rising.

Do not be afraid that honest intellectual work will necessarily diminish your religious earnestness. But I think that you may be satisfied with something less than " fourteen hours a day," whether you have wives or not. No man will have a right to call you indolent if, when you become ministers, you really work for eight or nine hours a day. As you grow older, and the claims of pastoral and public duties become more exacting, you will have reason to be grateful if, by putting your wife at your study door, with a bayonet on her shoulder to protect you from all intruders, you can make sure of even six or seven. Nor is it the amount of time that a man spends in his study that measures the amount of real work that he gets through. Some men do as much in five hours as other men of equal natural ability do in eight. For a man who is to be a preacher it is of great importance that he should acquire the habit of commanding his whole intellectual force whenever he wants to use it. If, by exerting all your strength, you can get through a piece of work in an hour and a half, and get through it well, you are injuring yourselves by spending two hours over it. I do not mean, of course, that you should care for nothing except the "pace" at which you can work; in trying for "pace" some men get "wild" and lose all their "form;" but vigorous habits of study will contribute to a vigorous habit of thinking and speaking.

There is an observation of the late Lord Lytton's which you will do well to remember while you are here, and which you may remember with advantage when you are in the ministry. In his judgment, "youths who are destined for active careers, or ambitious of distinction in such forms of literature as require freshness of invention or originality of thought, should avoid the habit of intense study for many hours at a stretch. There is a point in all tension of the intellect, beyond which effort is only a waste of strength. Fresh ideas do not readily spring up within a weary brain; and whatever exhausts the mind, not only enfeebles its power, but narrows its scope."[1] If any of you have been sunk into despair by what I have said about the enormous time which the Puritans

[1] "Caxtoniana," vol. ii. p. 327.

gave to their books, it may be a relief to you to hear another sentence of Lord Lytton's, which occurs very near to the passage I have quoted already:—" The man who has acquired the habit of study, though for only one hour every day in the year, and keeps to the one thing studied till it is mastered, will be startled to see the way he has made at the end of a twelvemonth." [1] But remember that everything depends upon the regularity with which you work, and upon the perseverance and the vigour.

NOTE TO PAGE 104.

After Lecture IV. was in type, I remembered that there was a passage in Hazlitt in which the charm of Old Books is charmingly celebrated. I quote the passage for its own sake, and also because what I have written on the same subject may have been partly suggested by it. Hazlitt's choice of books does not, however, seem to me very admirable.

"When I take up a work that I have read before (the oftener the better) I know what I have to expect. The satisfaction is not lessened by being anticipated. When the entertainment is altogether new, I sit down to it as I should to a strange dish—turn and pick out a bit here and there, and am in doubt what to think of the composition. There is a want of confidence and security to second appetite. New-fangled books are also like made-dishes in this respect, that they are generally little else than hashes and *rifaccimenti* of what has been served up entire and in a more natural state at other times. Besides, in thus turning to a well-known author, there is not only an assurance that my time will not be thrown away, or my palate nauseated with the most insipid or vilest trash, but I shake hands with, and look an old, tried, and valued friend in the face, compare notes, and chat the hours away. It is true, we form

---

[1] " Caxtoniana," vol. ii. p. 328.

dear friendships with such ideal guests, — dearer, alas! and more lasting, than those with our most intimate acquaintance. In reading a book which is an old favourite with me (say the first novel I ever read) I not only have the pleasure of imagination, and of a critical relish of the work, but the pleasures of memory added to it. It recalls the same feelings and associations which I had in first reading it, and which I can never have again in any other way. Standard productions of this kind are links in the chain of our conscious being. They bind together the different scattered divisions of our personal identity. They are landmarks and guides in our journey through life. They are pegs and loops on which we can hang up, or from which we can take down, at pleasure, the wardrobe of a moral imagination, the relics of our best affections, the tokens and records of our happiest hours. They are 'for thoughts and for remembrance.' They are like Fortunatus's Wishing-cap—they give us the best riches — those of fancy — and transport us, not over half the globe, but (which is better) over half our lives, at a word's notice.

"My father Shandy solaced himself with Bruscambille. Give me for this purpose a volume of "Peregrine Pickle" or "Tom Jones." Open either of them anywhere—at the Memoirs of Lady Vane, or the adventures at the masquerade with Lady Bellaston, or the disputes between Thwackum and Square, or the escape of Molly Seagrim, or the incident of Sophia and her muff, or the edifying prolixity of her aunt's lecture—and there I find the same delightful, busy, bustling scene as ever, and feel myself the same as when I was first introduced into the midst of it."— Hazlitt: Table Talk. "On reading Old Books," pp. 310, 311.

LECTURE V.

THE PREPARATION OF SERMONS.

GENTLEMEN,—When students for the ministry, or young preachers, have the opportunity of talking freely with a man who has been preaching for some years, they are almost certain to ask him what advice he can give them about the preparation of their sermons. In attempting to offer you some suggestions on this subject this afternoon, I do not think it necessary to begin by discussing the question whether it is better to preach extemporaneously, or to write your sermons and learn them, or to write them and read them; for, even if you write, you ought to have a great part of your preparation finished before the first sentence is put on paper. Rousseau said that when writing a love-letter, "you should begin without knowing what you are going to say, and end without knowing what you have said." That seems to me an excellent way of writing love-letters—though, perhaps, I am too old, and have too little sentiment left in me, for my opinion on the matter to have any authority—but I am sure that it is a very bad way of writing sermons.

I repeat that a great part of your preparation should

be finished before you begin to write; and, indeed, if you are to economise time and to preach effectively, a great part of your preparation should be finished— if I may venture to say it—before you begin to prepare. Let me explain what I mean.

I assume that you will read the Bible regularly— partly to master its contents for yourself, and partly to accumulate material for preaching. You will do well to read the Bible steadily through, but you should always have in hand some book which is likely to be fruitful in texts and topics for sermons. If, for instance, you give one half-hour in the morning to the Book of Numbers, you should give the next half-hour to one of the Gospels or one of the prophets; for, judging from my own experience, the Book of Numbers does not suggest many subjects on which it is worth while to preach to a Christian congregation. If you are reading the Book of Joshua—although this book is thought by some excellent people to be exceptionally rich in spiritual truth, and to be "the especial heritage of this generation"—you will do wisely to turn from the land-surveying and the wars of Joshua to the Psalms of David, or to one of the Epistles of St. John or St. Paul.

In reading the Bible for the purpose of accumulating material for sermons, you will, of course, read it with all the exegetical aids you happen to possess— your lexicons, your Greek and Hebrew concordances, and the best commentaries you have on your shelves. In your ordinary reading, perhaps, you will not find it of much use to read everything that half-a-dozen scholars have said on the book you are studying; there is necessarily a large amount of matter which is common to them all, and you will get weary of reading the same things over and over again. Read all that has been written on the book by one man, and consult the rest on points about which he has not satisfied you. When you go through the same book again, take another commentator for your principal guide. But whatever help of this kind you obtain, do not be satisfied with determining the meaning of a contested passage as you determine a contested election—by taking the interpretation which has most votes: think your own way through the difficulty. A great name is a strong reason for giving careful consideration to the opinion which it covers; but the greatest names can sometimes be alleged for opinions which are incredible.

Reading in this way, you will supply your minds with the raw material which you have to work up in your sermons—not merely with texts. The substance of our preaching has been given to us in a Divine revelation. This revelation is recorded in the Holy Scriptures. For us, therefore, the Bible is not merely a book of texts, but a text-book. It contains the truths we have to teach, the laws which we have to illustrate in their relations to the lives of our people, the divine promises by which we are to console them in trouble and to strengthen their faith in the love and power of God.

Read the Bible, as well as other books, with your note-sheets at hand. Whenever you meet with any historical illustration of a vice or a folly to which men are still tempted in our own days, or any noble and pathetic example of virtue, devotion, and zeal ; whenever you come across the statement of any truth concerning God, and His ways towards mankind, about which you have omitted to preach, or any moral precept on which you have omitted to insist, or any bright and pleasant region of spiritual thought which is likely to give animation and vigour to a weary and sorrowful heart, make a note of it. Half an hour's reading will often give you the substance of three or four sermons. Instead of hunting for a text or a subject when Sunday is coming near, you will only have to turn to the drawer in which your notes are kept, and you will find a score of sermons half ready. Two or three sets of notes will sometimes run naturally together into one discourse, and in using them you will have hardly anything to do except to prepare an introduction and a conclusion. Sometimes such light and fire will suddenly flash out of a sentence or a phrase that a whole sermon will come to you at once, and you will be able to transfer to your notes the rough outline of an effective discourse.

Your general reading and your theological reading may not be equally fruitful in subjects and materials for preaching, for the Bible is the great quarry of the preacher ; but even abstract theological speculations and controversies which have long been obsolete will sometimes originate lines of thought which will work easily and effectively into the plainest and most practical sermons. Always have your note-sheets on your desk. Whatever you are reading — theology, philosophy, history, poetry, fiction, biography, science — may at any moment give you something that will be of use in the pulpit. Sometimes you will get a subject for a sermon, sometimes a strong, epigrammatic statement of a great ethical truth which you will be glad to quote, sometimes a felicitous illustration. Do not be satisfied with recording a mere reference to the page of the book where you have found anything that you mean to use, or with simply indicating the subject or the line of thought which the book has suggested. Develop the illustration so that it may be almost ready to be transferred to your sermon when you want it. Indicate in your "notes" briefly, but distinctly, how the subject, or the line of thought, which has occurred to you should be treated. Write out the sentence at length which you mean to quote, and as you write you will probably think of an effective "setting" for it—something will occur to you that will naturally lead up to it.

It will also save you a great deal of trouble, and will help to preserve what I think Dr. Brooks called the "symmetry" of your preaching, if, at the beginning of the year, you draw up a list of a dozen or twenty subjects on which you think it desirable to preach before the year runs out. I shall have something to say about this in another lecture; for the present I will only ask you to consider whether what I fear is the very common practice of leaving the choice of subjects to mere chance, is not one of the chief reasons of the inefficiency of preaching as a means of religious and ethical instruction. If we have a list of subjects such as I have suggested, and refer to it now and then, thoughts will gradually crystallise round one subject after another until we shall find that we have a number of sermons almost ready to our hand.

In the choice of topics for sermons we should prefer those which in themselves have a strong moral and religious interest. Mr. Arnold's advice to a poet is worth remembering :—"I counsel him to choose for his subjects great actions ;" he does not deny "that the poetic faculty can and does manifest itself in treating the most trifling action, the most hopeless subject." "But," he adds, "it is a pity that power should be wasted ; and that the poet should be compelled to impart interest and force to his subject, instead of receiving them from it, and thereby doubling his impressiveness. There is, it has been excellently said, an immortal strength in the stories of great actions : the most gifted poet, then, may well be glad to supplement with it that mortal weakness, which in presence of the vast spectacle of life and the world, he must for ever feel to be his individual portion."[1] For the sake of the people, we are bound to choose subjects which stir the hearts of men and which touch

[1] Preface to "Poems." Second edition, 1854. Page vii.

the great duties, the great hopes and fears and sorrows of human life. For our own sakes, too, we should choose subjects of this kind. We are guilty of the most irrational conceit if we imagine that we shall be able, Sunday after Sunday, to invest with interest subjects which in themselves are uninteresting.

The quotation I have just made from Mr. Arnold reminds me of a verse of his, containing " a caution to poets," which also suggests a caution to preachers.

> " What poets feel not, when they make,
> A pleasure in creating,
> The world in *its* turn will not take
> Pleasure in contemplating." [1]

The application of this principle has its limits. I have already suggested the expediency of preparing a list of subjects at the beginning of the year, and you should make it a matter of conscience to exhaust the list during the year whether you feel any keen interest in the subjects or not. But your most effective sermons will be those in which you deal with aspects of truth and duty which have sovereign authority over your own life, which stir your imagination, fascinate your intellect, and inspire you with enthusiasm. If I may trust my own experience, we can hardly preach too often on any subject by which we ourselves are deeply moved. We may return to it Sunday after Sunday and month after month. As long as our own interest in it remains intense we shall preach about it in a way that will command the interest of our congregations.

[1] " New Poems." 1867. Page 159.

Never be afraid of saying the same thing over and over again, if you feel driven to say it by a strong sense of its importance. I suppose that most preachers who have any life and passion in them are under the benignant despotism of a succession of great truths and facts during successive periods of their ministry. For months they can hardly ever escape from the shadow and the glory of the death of the Lord Jesus Christ—the supreme crisis in the prolonged conflict between the righteousness and love of God and the sins and sorrows of the human race. Then, for months, the cross is almost forgotten, and the truth that the Christ who died is alive again, thrills them with a wonder and a joy as intense as the disciples felt when they first came to believe in the Resurrection. The freshness of this excitement passes away, and then, perhaps, they have a new and deeper sense of the awful majesty of Christ as the Judge of all mankind; and for weeks or months together they have so solemn an impression of the final account which every man must give of the deeds done in the body, that it seems to them as if a truth had been revealed to them which the Church had forgotten for centuries. At one time the infinite mercy of God in forgiving our sins for Christ's sake fills their thoughts day and night; at another they can think of nothing except the transcendent mystery of the life which is given to us in our regeneration; after this, they are penetrated with wonder at the greatness of the triumphs which, through the power of the Holy Ghost, the Christian man may achieve over sin; and then, perhaps, come bright and peaceful months in which the hope of the glory, honour, and immortality which are our inheritance in Christ becomes so strong and clear that heaven and earth appear to touch, and the fair city of God, which was seen by St. John in vision, seems as though it had already become the home and rest of the soul.

Now, I think it is quite safe to tell you that while you are "possessed" in this way by any great truth, you may preach about it again and again, and that the people will never get tired of listening to you. Only—remembering the great varieties of moral and spiritual conditions which exist in your congregation—you ought honestly to endeavour to interest yourself in other truths which may be necessary for the complete education and discipline of their moral and spiritual life.

I have spoken of the choice of "subjects" and of the choice of "texts;" but a text, if honestly selected, contains the subject on which you intend to preach, or, at least, fairly and naturally suggests the subject. To treat a text as a mere motto for a sermon is a practice which can very rarely be justified. If a minister does not intend to preach about what the text teaches or implies, he had better take no text at all. Whether it would be wise for you to do this must be determined by your own good sense. I do it myself occasionally, but I have been the minister of the same congregation for nearly five and twenty years, and can set aside the traditions of the pulpit without giving any offence. It may be that some congregations would not concede to a young preacher the same liberty.

When you take a text be sure that it is in the Bible. A friend of mine now dead—a very eminent preacher—once made what has been described to me as a very fine sermon on some words which he imagined were in the Book of Proverbs. On Sunday morning, before starting for church, he thought that it would be as well if he looked up the chapter in which he supposed that the words occurred. To his dismay the words were not to be found. He turned to his "Cruden," but Cruden failed him. He was still confident that the words were in the Book of Proverbs, and when the critical moment came for beginning to preach, he began by saying something to this effect: "You will remember, my friends, the words of the wisest of kings"—then he quoted his text and glided into his sermon as if he had innocently forgotten to say where the words of the wisest of kings occurred. Many a child in the congregation that afternoon hunted in vain through the Book of Proverbs and the Book of Ecclesiastes to discover the text of the morning's sermon. I think that my friend would have done better if he had warned the people that though he thought the words were Solomon's, he had not been able to find them, even with the help of a concordance. He discovered afterwards, I think, that the words were in one of the collects or prayers of the Anglican Prayer-book.

But it was not to warn you against accidents of this kind that I said you should make sure that your text is in the Bible. The text may be printed in our English version of the Holy Scriptures, and yet nothing corresponding to it may ever have been written by the hand of a Jewish scribe or of a Christian evangelist or apostle. It may stand for a corrupt reading which criticism has cancelled or modified; or it may be a false translation of the Hebrew or Greek. In either case the text is not really in the Bible at all, and if you treat it as though its integrity could not be challenged, you are not dealing fairly with your congregation.

Some preachers choose texts with apparently no other purpose than to display their own wonderful ingenuity. It is, no doubt, possible for a man to preach a very pathetic and earnest sermon on the words in Ezra i. 9: "nine and twenty knives," or on the description of the bedstead of Og king of Bashan, in Deut. iii. 11, "his bedstead was a bedstead of iron; is it not in Rabbath of the children of Ammon? nine cubits was the length thereof, and four cubits the breadth of it, after the cubit of a man."[1] But when I hear a man announce a text of this sort and watch the process by which he develops from it the doctrine of Justification by Faith, or the necessity of Regener-

[1] By way of caution to any of my young readers who may be enamoured of either of these texts, it may be as well to say that the "iron" of Og's bedstead was probably black basalt, and the "bedstead" a sarcophagus; and that it is very doubtful whether Ezra's "knives" were knives at all.

ation, or a theory of Divine Providence, or some interesting speculations on the millennium or the future blessedness of the righteous—and a sermon on "nine and twenty knives," or on Og's iron bedstead, may cover any one of these subjects as well as another—I always think of the tricks of those ingenious gentlemen who entertain the public by rubbing a sovereign between their hands till it becomes a canary, and drawing out of their coat sleeves half-a-dozen brilliant glass globes filled with water, and with four or five gold fish swimming in each of them. For myself, I like to listen to a good preacher, and I have no objection in the world to be amused by the tricks of a clever conjurer; but I prefer to keep the conjuring and the preaching separate: conjuring on Sunday morning, conjuring in church, conjuring with texts of Scripture, is not quite to my taste.

On the other hand there is considerable risk in choosing a text in which a great truth is stated with such sublimity and grandeur, or in which the deeper spiritual affections are expressed with such vehemence and energy, or in which there is so powerful an appeal to the imagination, that the text creates expectations which the sermon cannot fulfil. What can any man say after reading the words of St. John, "God is love"? What kind of a sermon do you lead your congregation to anticipate if you announce as your text the last two verses of the eighth chapter of the Epistle to the Romans, "I am persuaded, that neither death, nor life, nor angels, nor principalities, nor powers, nor things present, nor things to come, nor height, nor depth, nor any other creature, shall be able to separate us from the love of God which is in Christ Jesus our Lord"? What power of lyrical eloquence ought a preacher to have who ventures to write a sermon on Luke ii. 13, 14, "Suddenly there was with the angel a multitude of the heavenly host, praising God and saying, Glory to God in the highest, and on earth peace, good will toward men"?

There are texts of another kind, which I think are likely to disappoint us if we attempt to preach upon them, I remember hearing a sermon on the words, "We all do fade as a leaf." The little chapel in which it was delivered was in the Lake country: the fern on the hills and the woods below were taking their autumn tints of brown and gold. It was only necessary to step outside, and the beautiful country was a far more perfect and affecting sermon on the text than any mortal lips could deliver. For five or ten minutes, however, the preacher, who was a lady, succeeded admirably. She had caught the sentiment of the text, and her quiet gentle manner was in harmony with the pathos of her words. But then the vein was worked out, and the rest of the sermon was a series of colourless commonplaces. This was not the preacher's fault. The beauty and pathetic power of the text are derived from the perfection of the poetical form in which the brevity and decay of human life and strength and glory are expressed. A sermon on a text like that should be a prose poem, but the theme hardly admits of sufficient variations to permit the poem to extend to the ordinary length of a sermon. I doubt whether any poet could preserve the tone and sentiment of the original idea through a hundred lines, or even through fifty.

Are passages of this kind to be set aside by the preacher as useless? Is he never to avail himself in the pulpit of the most sublime, the most animating, the most touching, the most beautiful words of prophets, psalmists, and apostles? You can hardly imagine that I mean to offer you such discouraging advice as this.

The true course, as I venture to think, is obvious. Passages which we hardly dare to take as texts may contribute to our sermons their most effective and impressive lines of thought. Had the lady preacher of whom I was speaking just now, selected as the text of her sermon some passage in which the frailty of man is expressed with less poetic beauty, she might have gradually prepared her congregation for the striking and pathetic reflections which had occurred to her on the words — "We all do fade as a leaf." And so, if your imagination is excited by any of the details in St. John's description of the New Jerusalem; if you have taken fire at the words, "the street of the city was pure gold," and "the twelve gates were twelve pearls;" or if some bright and pleasant fancies have clustered round the beautiful words in an earlier chapter of the same book—"there was a rainbow round about the throne, in sight like unto an emerald"

—although I think that it would be perilous to take any of these words as the text of a sermon, there is no need that your thoughts about them should be wasted. Take some quieter and less dazzling words as a text, and gradually work your way to the beauty and glory which you have found in these imaginative passages.

The great and noble texts of which I was speaking just now—texts which contain a promise too large for any sermon to fulfil—may be dealt with in the same way. If they have moved your own heart deeply, if they have given you vigorous and lofty thoughts, which you are eager to use, take a text which excites less expectation, and so construct your sermon that it shall gradually lead up to the heights of truth, to the exulting hopes, the glowing passion with which your soul has been thrilled.

These suggestions are, of course, not intended as an inflexible law. There are occasions on which we may preach on the most glorious passages which are to be found in the Old Testament or the New; there are moods in which no words are too pathetic or too animating or too startling for us to preach about them; but as a rule I think it is safe to avoid texts that are very sublime, very striking, or very remarkable for their imaginative beauty.

When you have chosen your text and your topic, how are you to begin to prepare? If your "notes" serve you well, you will already have in hand a considerable amount of material; but whether you have little or much, you should first of all come to a clear understanding with yourself about the precise object of your sermon.

What is the sermon to do? The answer to this question determines the whole method of preparation.

Is it your principal intention to prove some Christian doctrine, to support the teaching of a particular text by appealing to the concurrent authority of other parts of Holy Scripture ?—then your line of preparation is clear. If you do not happen to have in hand, as the result of your previous studies, an organised statement of the Scripture evidence—direct and indirect—of the truth on which you are about to preach, you must rely on your general knowledge of the contents of the Bible, and you must hunt up the proofs you want, and carefully verify them.

Is it your intention to state and explain some truth which you have reason to suppose is not generally understood ? Then you may be greatly helped by thinking of two or three members of your congregation who are least likely to understand it, and you should consider by what lines of thought and by what class of illustrations you would be able to make the truth clear to them if you were talking to them in private. If in your congregation there are persons who have grave misconceptions of the truth, you will be tempted to begin by attacking and exposing what you suppose to be their mistakes. This is the easy way of trying to set them right, but it is not the effective way. Men will not part with what they have, until you give them something better. The attack provokes defence. Most people are very unwilling to find out for themselves that they have been in the wrong; they are still more unwilling to let any one else prove to them that they have been in the wrong. Develop your own conception of the truth first—not aggressively, with your teeth set, your hand clenched, and your war-paint on; but quietly and modestly. Consider what kind of proof will satisfy the minds of those who are least likely to accept your teaching; look for illustrations that shall be adjusted to their temper and habits; try to discover how you can secure for your own position the moral and religious sympathies of those who are intellectually opposed to it; make some practical and manifestly wholesome application of point after point as your thought moves on; and you will find that a sermon is gradually growing which will make the truth plain to those who had not understood it at all, and will correct the mistakes of those who had formed a false conception of it.

Perhaps your principal object is practical; you want to get the people to discharge some duty which they neglect, or to break with some sin. If you have reason to believe that they have no clear understanding of the nature of the duty, or that they do not believe that the sin is forbidden by the law of Christ, your first endeavour must be to instruct their consciences; and until the necessary instruction has been given, your appeals and warnings, no matter how solemn, vehement, and passionate, will have no effect. You will then consider what motives will most powerfully influence the particular class of persons who are neglecting the duty on which you are insisting, or who are committing the positive sin from which you are trying, with God's good help, to rescue them.

Or your intention may be to strengthen some religious affection, to confirm the trust of your congregation in God's infinite mercy, to deepen their reverence for the Divine Majesty, to give them nobler conceptions of the power and glory of God, to alleviate sorrow and anxiety by confirming their faith in the compassion and pity of Him who knoweth our frame, and remembereth that we are dust; or you want to inspire their zeal for the kingdom of Christ with new fervour; or to give larger breadth and greater tenderness to their Christian charity. If this is your object, you will not be looking vaguely to the right and to the left for any original and brilliant and eloquent things which your subject may happen to suggest; but you will consider how the subject on which you are intending to preach can be presented so as to produce the definite impression which you desire.

The general principle which I have been trying to illustrate is very simple and very obvious; it is one of those commonplaces which I told you were to make up the whole substance of this course of lectures; but precisely because it is a commonplace I attach great importance to it. I believe that many young preachers, when they sit down to prepare a sermon, start like Abraham, who "went out, not knowing whither he went." Or perhaps it would be truer to say that for half an hour or an hour they do not start at all, but look idly round their subject, and wonder whether they will be able to make anything of it. At last, by some accident, they find what looks like a path, and after trying it they find that it leads nowhere, and so they come back to the place where they began. The preacher who has a definite end to reach, rarely loses any of the time which he gives to preparation; he sees in the distance the point to which he has to travel, and he either finds or makes a road to it.

I wonder whether you know anything on this side of the Atlantic of the terrible difficulty which we Englishmen experience in thinking of something to say when we are making a formal call on persons who are almost strangers to us. If I may judge from the Americans whom it has been my pleasure to meet in different parts of the world, you have far greater freedom and vivacity and inventiveness in conversation than we have, and, perhaps, the difficulty to which I am referring never troubles you. We open the conversation, as a matter of course, by talking of the weather. We inform the lady or gentleman on whom we are calling that there has been a great deal of rain, or that the east wind is very trying, or that the unusual dryness of the season has made the dust extremely unpleasant. Then we begin to feel a little nervous, and wonder what we shall say next. We think ourselves very fortunate if we happen to discover that the lady was at a concert the night before, or that the gentleman is going to Scotland the next day. We are still more happy if we learn that either of them has been suffering from toothache for a fortnight, so that we can dilate on the dexterity of our favourite dentist; or if we discover that one of the young gentlemen of the house has lately had an accident with his bicycle and broken his leg, or that he fell into the river a week ago and was half drowned. Then we can get on merrily enough till the time comes when we can with decency rise to go. If none of these fruitful subjects offer themselves we soon become very miserable, and we sympathise keenly with Anna Gascoigne in " Daniel Deronda," who said, " I am not at all clever, and I never know what to say. It seems so useless to say what everybody knows, and I can think of nothing else, except what papa says."

But if we wish to secure some definite object, the difficulty of " making conversation " vanishes at once. If we want to persuade the lady to join a musical society, or to become one of the patronesses of a flower show; if we want the gentleman to vote for the Liberal candidate for the borough, or to go on the committee of a hospital, or to become a member of a new club, or to subscribe a couple of guineas a year to an orphan asylum, we have plenty to say, especially if there is any hesitation to be overcome, or if there are any misconceptions to be corrected. It is also true that while a preacher who simply wants to find something good and sensible to say to his congregation for half an hour or forty minutes, may be driven to his wits' ends to think of anything that is worth saying, a preacher who wants to get them to understand something which they do not understand clearly, or to do something, or to leave something undone, will find that the object he wants to gain will suggest what he ought to say, and the difficulty of preparing a sermon will be greatly lightened.

You have noticed, perhaps, that I have said nothing about preparing "the plan" of the sermon, or what in some books on preaching is grimly called "the skeleton." Some preachers begin with their "plan." They think that it is their first business to "divide" their subject or their text; and having constructed their divisions, they fill them up as best they can. When I was at college we had each to read a sermon in class about twice in the session; but we had to prepare "plans"—with divisions and subdivisions—about once in three weeks. A sermon might take three or four evenings to prepare; but a "plan" was not supposed to take more than half an hour, and I suspect that many a plan was thrown off in five minutes. If the "plan" looked promising it was sometimes developed into a sermon. I have heard that it is the custom in some colleges for the homiletical professor to announce a text, and to require the students of his class in turn to give him, off-hand, the plan of a sermon upon it. Whether any practice of this kind exists at Yale I do not know. If it does, I have no doubt that your professor could give you excellent reasons for it as a class exercise. But it is my impression that the habit of making the "plan" of a sermon first and getting the materials afterwards is likely to have an injurious effect on a man's preaching. The "plan" of a sermon is the order in which the materials are arranged, and it seems to me that the reasonable method is to arrange the materials when you have got them to arrange—not before.

When you are about to build a house, you tell your architect what you want—how large the dining-room and the drawing-room must be, what kind of a library he must give you, and what aspect you would like these rooms to have; and you tell him how many bedrooms you want. When he knows for what he has to arrange, he prepares his plans and his elevation; and, if he understands his profession, his plans and elevation are governed by the number and size and uses of the rooms which are required. It is this which makes one of the chief differences between good and bad architecture, between architecture which is dead and formal, and architecture which has life, freedom, and vigour in it. A poor architect designs the outside of his building first, prepares his ground-plan and elevation, and then does the best he can in arranging the interior. A good architect begins with the inside: asks, first of all, what the contents of the building are to be, and lets these determine everything. I think that there is a similar difference between good and bad architecture in sermons. Make your "plan" first, and your sermon is in great danger of being formal; you will have to exclude some of the best materials that come to you; or you will fling them down into the Introduction, because there is no place for them anywhere else, just as we are in the habit of leaving our heavy luggage in the hall of an hotel, because we cannot get it into the bedrooms.

In building a house, an architect is sometimes under restraints which prevent him from working on what he knows is the right principle. If the house is to stand in a row, he may be obliged to make the outside of it precisely like the outside of the houses that stand to the right and to the left of it. He has no scope for his genius. Formality is his doom, and he must submit to it. But a preacher is under no such restraints. Every sermon stands by itself, in its own grounds, and may be built just as the preacher pleases. If the sermon is full of sentiment and fancy, it may be a pleasant cottage, with lawns and flower gardens round it, and with windows open to the sun and air, and with roses and honeysuckles growing about the porch. If it is an attack on some grave speculative error or on some evil practice, it may be a fort with walls of granite, pierced here and there for a rifle to be thrust through, defended by earthworks, and mounted with heavy guns. The mischief is that some preachers build all their sermons as though they were to stand side by side in a street, and as though it were necessary to make the front of number 264 precisely the same as the front of number 265. Whatever there may be inside, the outside conforms to an almost invariable model. The door is always in the same place, the rows of windows are faultlessly uniform, there is the same number of floors in every one of them between the foundation and the roof—three principal divisions, with three sub-divisions under each, and then an application: they are all nine-roomed houses, with attics on the top. This comes, I think, of making the plan first.

There is another evil which is incident to this practice. Having made your plan, you have then to fill up every one of the little logical or rhetorical squares with argument, sentiment, explanation, or appeal. Your thinking is done " to order," and the result is not likely to be very satisfactory. The work is almost certain to be uneven. Some of the thought will be forced and some will be tame. Your most vigorous thinking will perhaps come in your first division, and the rest of the sermon will be weak and ineffective. You should have two plans: the first, a plan to guide your own thought while accumulating your material; the second, a plan for arranging the material when you have accumulated it.

Should the divisions of the second plan be announced? In England most Nonconformist preachers always announce what are sometimes called the "heads" of their sermons. Among the clergy of the Established Church I believe that the practice is less common. When the sermon is mainly didactic, when it consists of a series of motives to enforce some duty, or of a carefully organised procession of proofs in support of some doctrinal or ethical proposition, the announcement of the divisions will probably help your congregation to understand and to remember what you are saying. But I see no more reason for always announcing the divisions of a sermon than for always announcing the divisions of a speech. If the thoughts of the sermon are well massed, if land and water, earth and sky, are definitely separated from each other, instead of being left in the confusion of chaos, the sermon will be effective at the time, and the main points of it will be remembered afterwards, whether the divisions are announced or not.

There are some obvious disadvantages in announcing them. The sermon is in danger of becoming a series of short sermons, with the divisions for separate texts; and there is sometimes a great deal of trouble in making a natural and easy transition from one division to another.

If the "heads" are announced it will sometimes be expedient to announce them at the close of the successive parts of the sermon to which they belong, instead of at the beginning. A few months ago I heard this done very effectively by one of the most eloquent of the High Anglican clergy — Mr. Body. He was preaching on a well-known text in Isaiah: "It shall come to pass in the last days that the mountain of the Lord's house shall be established in the top of the mountains, and shall be exalted above the hills; and all nations shall flow unto it." His subject was the Power of the Church. In his Introduction, after a rather fanciful exposition of the text, he gave a glowing description of the triumphs which the Christian Church has already won over the hearts and lives of mankind. He effected his transition to the main argument of his discourse by asking, How have these triumphs been won? What is the secret of this force which enables the Church to subdue men of every race and of every variety of culture and civilisation? To these questions he replied by another, What is it that men chiefly need? Then followed a series of very vivid illustrations of the universal consciousness of guilt. And is mercy possible? Yes, he answered. God has come from heaven to earth to atone for the sins of men. He then gave a noble and pathetic statement of the doctrine of the Atonement—an atonement effected for all men, in all countries, and all ages. But to make known to mankind the infinite mercy of God revealed through Christ is one of the chief functions of the Church. Her message is received with wonder and joy, the sinful are drawn to her feet. The *first* element therefore of the Church's power is this—*She is Evangelical.* But when the soul has learnt to trust in Christ for the pardon of sin, it is eager, he said, to learn all that can be known about God and about the will of God. What shall it believe? Can any of the sects, he asked, reply to that question with confidence? He told us that men whose love for Christ seems equally fervent teach conflicting doctrines, and differ as to the authority and meaning of the sacred rites of the Christian faith. The Independent agrees with the Church as to the perpetual obligation of Infant Baptism and the Lord's Supper; the Baptist refuses to baptise infants; the members of the Society of Friends will baptise neither infants nor adults, nor will they celebrate the Lord's Supper. This line of observation was developed with great vivacity, but with great kindliness; and then he reminded us of the Church, with its ancient creeds, and of the authority with which it claims to speak as the living representative of the great Society founded by Christ and His apostles. He closed this part of the sermon by saying that the *second* element of the power of the Church is this—*She is Dogmatic.* The rest of the sermon it is unnecessary to quote.

This method has the advantage of stimulating and suspending curiosity. When a preacher begins by announcing the proposition which he intends to prove or to illustrate, the congregation will generally see a straight piece of road before them, and will feel that their attention may be relaxed till the next turn comes. Sometimes, however, the proposition will be misunderstood, sometimes it will provoke antagonism. The misunderstanding will be obviated if the illustration comes first and the proposition afterwards; and if the proof is given before the proposition is stated, the antagonism may not arise.

But no general rule can be given. A preacher may sometimes see that he will excite curiosity by stating his divisions before explaining, proving, or enforcing them. We must judge for ourselves. What I am anxious to contend for is variety and freedom.

When you have got your materials together and arranged them, I think you should ask whether your sermon will contain an adequate amount of positive Christian truth ; whether what you have prepared is governed and inspired by a recognition of the true relations of the human race to God as those relations are illustrated in the revelation which has been made to us through Christ ; whether your sermon will satisfy the apostolic conception of what the preaching of the gospel ought to be ; whether it is likely to secure any of the great ends for which the Christian ministry is established, and the particular end which you had proposed to yourself in preparing it; whether you are leaving anything unsaid that as a Christian preacher you are bound to say ; whether the spirit of the sermon will be in harmony with the mind of Christ.

You may then look at your materials from another point of view. Is the sermon likely to be monotonous in tone and colour ? Will it be sufficiently varied to be interesting to all sorts of people ? You may consider whether the subject has any pathetic aspects which you have overlooked ; whether you have brought it into a sufficiently close relation to the conscience and to the common lives of men ; whether, with the materials you have prepared, the subject will be lit up with imagination or fancy ; whether there will be a sufficient glow of feeling.

Do not suppose that I mean you to manufacture an imaginative paragraph, or a pathetic paragraph, or a humorous paragraph : to do this will make your sermon very false and artificial. But to secure interest and effectiveness, you ought to try to appeal to as many elements of human nature as possible; and in looking through your rough notes you will sometimes find that there are the germs of imaginative, pathetic, impassioned, or humorous passages which you have omitted to develop, and which might be developed with great advantage.

In this review of what you have prepared you will make sure of saying—and saying clearly—the main thing about your subject that ought to be said and that you want to say. Dr. Duncan—Rabbi Duncan—after listening to a sermon, declared that "the idea of the preacher was in the sentence *after the last.*"

You will then consider what ought to be said in your Introduction, unless, indeed, you believe with Pascal, who I am inclined to think was right, that "the last thing a man finds out when he is writing a book is how to begin," and in that case you will postpone preparing the Introduction until you have determined how the sermon is to end.

The Introduction is one of the great perplexities of young preachers. Very often they spend an amount of strength upon it which would be far better used later in the sermon. The style and size of the porch ought to bear some proportion to the style and size of the house. My late friend M. de Félice, one of the most eminent of modern preachers among the Protestants of France, once said to a colleague of his, M. Pédézert, "I want half an hour's preliminary conversation with my hearers." "Then," replied M. Pédézert, "you begin just when others are finishing." M. de Félice, I believe, generally preached for an hour and a half. Even in his case, half an hour's "preliminary conversation," in the shape of an elaborate Introduction, was a sufficiently serious encroachment on the time at his disposal; but for a man who preaches for only five and thirty minutes to have an Introduction of a quarter of an hour, is a far graver mistake. In listening to the ostentatious preparations which some preachers think it necessary to make before they fairly get into their sermon, which too often proves to be a very poor one after all, one is inclined to ask, in the words of Robert Browning—

> " But why such long prolusion and display,
> Such turning and adjustment of the harp;
> And taking it upon your breast at length,
> Only to speak dry words across its strings?"

The Introduction should be as brief as possible. As a rule, it should spring directly and naturally out of the text; that is, if the text is announced first. If you want to say something before you refer to your text, keep back your text till you have said it. But the best advice I can give you is to get to work as soon as you can. If your text requires explanation, explain it; if not, do not waste your time by explaining it.

The time which most young preachers devote to the preparation of the Introduction would be far better spent on the close, or what our fathers used to call the *Application*, of their sermons. About this all authorities are agreed. An English preacher of the last generation used to say that he cared very little what he said the first half-hour, but that he cared a very great deal what he said the last fifteen minutes. I remember reading many years ago an address delivered to students by Mr. Henry Ward Beecher, in which he gave a very striking account of the sermons of Jonathan Edwards. Mr. Beecher said that in the elaborate doctrinal part of Jonathan Edwards's sermons the great preacher was only getting his guns into position; but that in his " applications " he opened fire on the enemy. There are too many of us, I am afraid, who take so much time in getting our guns " into position," that we have to finish without firing a shot. We say that we leave the truth to do its own work. We trust to the hearts and consciences of our hearers to "apply it." Depend upon it, gentlemen, this is a great and fatal mistake.

Sometimes, indeed, we may preach a sermon which is " application " from the first sentence to the last, as an eloquent friend of mine once delivered a speech an hour long, which was enthusiastically described as " all peroration." Mr. Finney's sermons were not unfrequently of this kind. I do not mean that he " perorated " all through, but that the whole sermon was "application." I heard him very often during his visit to England when I was a student, and it seemed to me that the iron chain of the elaborate theological argument which sometimes constituted the substance

of his discourse—an argument on Free Will, or on the
Evil of Sin, or on the Moral Necessity which obliged
God to punish Sin—was fastened to an electric battery : every link of the chain as you touched it gave
you a moral shock ; but even in Mr. Finney's sermons
the supreme impression usually came at the end ; the
effect was cumulative.

The principle on which the closing passages of
our sermons should be prepared is obvious. Having
demonstrated some Christian truth, or having explained some Christian duty, we have to ask ourselves
how we can project the truth into the very depths of the
thought and life of our congregation, so that they shall
never lose it; how we can constrain them to discharge
the duty. We may secure these ends in many ways.
Even if our principal object is to set or keep the
faith of the people right, the truth will be most
firmly enthroned in the intellect if we invoke the
alliance of the conscience and of the spiritual affections, or if we exhort the people to the discharge of
the special duty which the truth imposes upon all who
receive it. Sometimes, on the other hand, the living
authority of the truth will be felt most vividly, and
its shining glory will be most clearly seen, if it is
suddenly contrasted with the antagonistic error. Or
if it is our object to strengthen the religious affections
—the gratitude, the love, the trust, the hope, the joy,
which the truth inspires—we may often succeed by
giving free expression to the feeling and passion which
the truth has enkindled in our own hearts. If we are

enforcing a duty, we may crown all that we have said by some vivid historical illustration of the beauty and nobleness of the particular excellence on which we are insisting, or of the shamefulness and baseness of the opposite vice. Or we may give heart and courage to those who may think that the duty is above their strength, by recalling with exulting confidence the great promises of God. Or we may appeal to fear or to hope, or to the authority of Christ, which no Christian heart can resist. We shall do well to study the various methods which successful preachers have followed in this part of their sermons. Original methods of reaching the heart and the conscience and influencing the will are of far more value to a preacher who wants to do his work well than originality of any other kind.

There are one or two suggestions of a general character which I should like to offer before I close.

Never be afraid of making your explanations of any truth, or fact, or duty, too simple and elementary. One of the most charming popular preachers and speakers that I ever knew, said to me once that he always took it for granted that the people knew nothing about the subject on which he was speaking to them. A few months ago, in a passage of a great speech on the Eastern Question delivered at Birmingham, Mr. John Bright showed that, consciously or unconsciously, he spoke on the same principle. He explained the precise position of Constantinople on the Bosphorus, and described the Sea of Marmora and the Dardanelles. I did not happen to be in Birmingham when the speech was delivered, and while reading it in a railway carriage in the north of England the next morning, I wondered whether for once Mr. Bright's oratorical instinct had failed him, and whether the audience had showed any signs of impatience while they were listening to this elementary information. When I got home my friends told me that this passage of the speech was listened to with the closest attention. Mr. Bright was right, as usual, and he had given me another illustration, in addition to the innumerable illustrations which he had given me before, of the true method of addressing great audiences.

The thoughts of ordinary men on most things not connected with their own profession are very indefinite. Large numbers of persons, who have been accustomed to read the Bible and to listen to preaching all their lives, have the loosest possible acquaintance with the details of biblical history, and their conceptions of doctrinal truth are extremely vague. They are grateful to any man who will make their knowledge of the external facts of Holy Scripture definite, and who will give sharpness and firmness to the outlines of their conceptions of truth.

Young preachers are afraid to say the same thing over and over again. Mr. Finney, in his Autobiography, quotes what a judge in your Supreme Court once said to him on this subject, and it deserves your careful consideration. "Ministers," he said, "do not exercise good sense in addressing the people. They are afraid of repetition. Now, if lawyers should take such a course, they would ruin themselves and their cause. When I was at the bar," he added, "I used to take it for granted, when I had before me a jury of respectable men, that I should have to repeat over my main positions about as many times as there were persons in the jury-box. I learned that unless I did so, illustrated, and repeated, and turned the main points over—the main points of law and of evidence—I should lose my cause."[1] The judge was right. We should all preach more effectively if, instead of tasking our intellectual resources to say a great many things in the same sermon, we tried to say a very few things in a great many ways.

[1] "Finney's Autobiography," p. 85.

LECTURE VI.

EXTEMPORANEOUS PREACHING AND STYLE.

GENTLEMEN,—About the comparative advantages of preaching from a manuscript and preaching extemporaneously, I have some difficulty in speaking. It seems to me that the overwhelming weight of the argument is on the side of extemporaneous preaching; but I have very rarely the courage to go into the pulpit without carrying with me the notes of my sermon, and occasionally I read every sentence from the first to the last.

The contrast between my theory of preaching and my practice is in this respect very glaring; but I had better avail myself of this opportunity of saying that in many other respects the contrast, if less glaring, is not less real. Some of the worst faults, some of the most fatal mistakes, which I have entreated you to avoid, are the faults and the mistakes which I have found it most difficult to avoid myself; and the bitterness with which I may have spoken of these vices has come from the soreness of heart with which I remember the extent to which they have impaired the power of my own preaching, and from the resentment I feel against them as my own persistent enemies—resentment which has been intensified by prolonged and not very successful struggles to escape from their power. The methods of work which I recommend to you are not mere theoretical suggestions. I have tested their value; but some of them I began to try too late. I shall be grateful if the experience I have acquired from my own failures contributes anything to your success.

It is not every man that appears in the pulpit without his manuscript who is an extemporaneous preacher. In Scotland and in France, where the people regard the " paper " with horror, it is a common practice for ministers to write their sermons and to learn them by heart — clause after clause, sentence after sentence, paragraph after paragraph. Some men, without any attempt to learn what they have written, reproduce it with hardly the variation of a single phrase. I have heard of eminent preachers who are able to compose and to retain in their memory long discourses without putting pen to paper. None of these are extemporaneous preachers.

On the other hand it is not necessary, in order to preach extemporaneously, that we should choose our text as we go into the pulpit, and say what happens to come first. M. Coquerel puts it admirably when he says that the extemporaneous preacher " knows what he is going to say, but does not know how he will say it."[1] Even this definition may require some

[1] "Observations Pratiques sur la Prédication." Athanase Coquerel. Page 193.

qualification. A man may be fairly said to preach extemporaneously although he may have in his mind a few strong epigrammatic sentences with which he intends to close and to clinch some passages in his sermon; and who, in thinking over an illustration which requires vivid or delicate treatment, has hit upon the felicitous phrases in which he means to clothe it.

A friend of mine now dead, who was a very effective preacher and speaker, used to talk over his sermons and his speeches, before he delivered them, with any one he happened to meet. He was a very busy man, but was always ready for a gossip: his gossip was part of his work. How often he has caught me in one of the most crowded streets of Birmingham, or on the steps of the Public Library, and put to me a thought or an argument or an illustration which he meant to use in a sermon on the following Sunday morning, or in a speech in the Town Hall the next night! Perhaps the idea had just occurred to him, and then he would develop it briefly and in outline, and make it grow while he was talking. Perhaps he had already tried it with some one he had met earlier in the day, and in that case the passage had taken a certain finish: he revised it while he repeated it. It was his custom to write his sermons and speeches, though he rarely used any notes; but it is my impression that he had got not only all his main thoughts, but the very best words he could find for expressing them, before he wrote a line.

A member of the House of Commons was telling me a few weeks ago that one of our famous political orators prepares in the same way. Before he makes a great speech, said my friend, he talks over all the points with every man he sees, and if he can talk to nobody else, he will talk to his gardener. Sentence after sentence, one epigram after another, gets into shape in this way.

Great mistakes are made about the habits of orators and preachers. I remember being struck very powerfully when I was a student by a picturesque description of the way that Bossuet prepared his sermons. The writer — I quite forget who it was—said that Bossuet used to sit at his table for a short time in perfect stillness, while with an eagle eye he glanced over the whole extent of the subject on which he was meditating ; that gradually he became excited, and that then he dashed down ten or a dozen sentences, indicating the principal lines along which, when he was in the pulpit, his superb genius was to travel ; and that when these were written the preparation was over. Very picturesque, rather melodramatic, and, if intended as a description of Bossuet's uniform practice, absolutely false ! Sometimes, it is true, Bossuet wrote very brief notes ; sometimes he wrote at length, but wrote rapidly ; sometimes he wrote with great care, and subjected what he had written to exact revision. His method of preparation varied with the varying leisure at his disposal, and with the varying subjects on which he preached. And yet he may be almost described as an extemporaneous preacher, for he does not seem to have been in the habit of reproducing with any close accuracy what he had written. His preparation had made him master of himself and of his subject; he watched his congregation; he worked out lines of thought which, in his manuscript, he had barely suggested, if he saw that they told; he sometimes threw aside, when he was face to face with the people, what M. Gandar calls " the scholastic subtleties, which the theologian, in his study, could hardly avoid ";[1] he took fire as he spoke, and he did not try to repress the flame.

Lacordaire, if we may trust M. Montalembert, who was likely to be perfectly informed about his friend's habits, was an extemporaneous preacher in the strictest sense, and his extemporaneous power, in M. Montalembert's judgment, was a principal element of his effectiveness. In preparing his great Conferences he took but very little time, but while he worked the intellectual effort was intense. He wrote nothing. The Conferences were taken down in shorthand: the reports were submitted to him the next day, and the corrections which he made were very inconsiderable. Lacordaire, with all his magnificent powers, did not, as M. Montalembert acknowledges, escape altogether from the perils which beset the extemporary speaker. Sometimes he was too emphatic, sometimes too declamatory. It must be ascribed, I suppose, to his neglect of writing, that his

[1] " Bossuet : Orateur." By E. Gandar. Page xlv.

logic was sometimes weak and sometimes confused; that he often disturbed and even distressed his congregation by stating with such force an objection which he meant to answer, that, when the answer came, it appeared inadequate. Perhaps, too, it was because he prepared the substance only, and not the form of his sermons, that he too rarely achieved the perfect beauty which comes from perfect simplicity.[1]

These are the faults into which the extemporaneous preacher—no matter what may be his genius—is almost certain to be betrayed. He may do very much to avoid them if he writes carefully, though without any intention of recalling, when he is in the pulpit, the precise language in his manuscript.

The advantages of writing and reading are obvious. The preacher who goes to church with his sermon in his pocket is sure of having something to say. He escapes the anxiety with which many of the best extemporaneous preachers are tormented every Friday and Saturday. My predecessor, John Angell James, usually preached without his manuscript, though he nearly always wrote his sermons. While I was a student he had to preach on what is regarded by us as a great occasion in connection with the London Missionary Society. He happened to tell me three weeks before the sermon was to be delivered that he intended to read it, and I ventured, rather presumptuously, to remonstrate with him. "Why

---

[2] See "Le Père Lacordaire." By Le Comte de Montalembert. Second edition, pp. 143-145.

shouldn't I read?" he asked. "Because you are never so effective when you read," I replied. He gave me an odd look, and said, "·Well now, I'll tell you how it is. If I preach without reading I shall be miserable for three weeks—miserable till I am in the pulpit ; if I read, I shall be quite happy till I begin to preach, though I shall be miserable till I finish." The old man's reason for using his manuscript was not to be answered ; and I suppose that there are many preachers who, if they did not read, would soon be worn away by the anxiety and dread with which they would anticipate their Sunday's work.

It must also be conceded that in sermons in which clearness and precise accuracy in the statement of truth are of special importance, the man who reads is likely to have a great advantage. Language is a difficult instrument to master, and even the ablest speakers and those who have had the longest practice cannot always command at the moment the simplest and most transparent expression of their thought. This is especially true when they are dealing with unfamiliar lines of speculation. The written sermon is also likely to be most successful in the clear and orderly development of an elaborate argument.

Nor is it fair to say that those who read their sermons show a distrust of the aid of the Holy Spirit. Our self-distrust, our dependence upon Divine teaching and aid, may be just as perfect when we are writing as when we are speaking. I do not accept the superstition which implies that the Spirit of God is with us in the pulpit and not in the study. Those who argue that it is a sign of want of faith to write and to read, ought also to protest against making any preparation for preaching at all. Verbal inspiration is not claimed; it is for the substance of his sermon that the preacher is to rely on the illumination of the Spirit of God; and the man who prepares the substance of his sermon and not the form, is therefore open to precisely the same charge as the man who prepares its form as well as its substance. So far, indeed, as this argument is concerned, I think that the preacher who writes his sermons and reads them is in a rather better position than the man who prepares the general outlines of his thoughts without writing. They both prepare the substance of their sermons, for which we are told that they ought to rely on the illumination of the Holy Ghost, and therefore they are both equally guilty of distrust; but the one who does not write is also guilty of presumption, for he relies on the inspiration of the Holy Ghost for the language he will want, though for this reliance it is admitted that there is no adequate ground. The whole argument is preposterous and fanatical. If carried to its logical issue it would require us to go into the pulpit without selecting a text.

There is one advantage on the side of writing and reading sermons, which is rarely mentioned. Extemporaneous sermons, as Hooker says, "spend their life in their birth, and may have public audience but once."[1] If a man writes and reads he can preach his old ser-

[1] Hooker: "Ecclesiastical Polity." Book v. cap. xxi.

mons over again, and preach them effectively. When ministers remove to a new congregation, I suppose that they have no scruples about preaching sermons which they have preached before ; but I can see no sufficient reason for not preaching sermons a second or a third time to the same congregation. Indeed, after an interval of seven or eight years, though we may be preaching in the same pulpit, we are not preaching to the same congregation. Many of the people have died; some have removed to other churches or to other parts of the country ; new people have taken their places ; children have become young men and women; young men and women who were uninterested in the sermon when it was first preached have had their moral and intellectual interest in religious truth awakened, and will listen to it with eager attention. If you write a sermon on any of those great topics to which you are bound to recur frequently—on the Divinity of our Lord Jesus Christ, for instance, or on the Personality of the Holy Spirit, or on the nature of Regeneration, or on the Protestant doctrine of Justification, or on the principles which will determine the judgment of men at the last day ;—if the substance of the sermon is the result of reading and thought extending over many months ; if you think that the statement of the scriptural proof of the doctrine is clear and full and strong ; if the arrangement satisfies you ; if the whole discussion is as complete and effective as you can make it—I think that you will waste a good piece of work if you use it only once and then throw it aside. Some of the people — perhaps many of them—will recognise it as an old sermon; but your congregation will be a very remarkable one if there are more than a very few persons who will remember the contents of it so perfectly that it will not do them good to hear the sermon again. The Rev. Caleb Morris, who, thirty years ago, was one of the ablest and most fascinating preachers among the English Congregationalists, was obliged, some time before his death, to resign his pastorate on account of ill-health; but he continued to conduct a religious service in his own drawing-room, at which twenty or thirty persons were present. I have heard that, after reading the Scriptures and offering prayer, he sometimes examined his little congregation on the sermon of the preceding Sunday. If he found that they did not remember it very well he preached it over again. I am not sure that I can commend Mr. Morris's practice to your imitation, but there was surely a great deal of good sense in it. If it became common it would considerably lighten our labours in the preparation of our sermons.

Nor is it only sermons which contain an elaborate proof and illustration of the great central doctrines of the Christian faith which may be preached over again. Ten years ago, certain aspects of ethical and religious truth and duty exerted exceptional power over my own moral and spiritual life: five years earlier, certain other aspects of truth had the same ascendency, and ruled me with the same authority. These particular truths or particular aspects of truth do not seem to me less important now than they were when they haunted me day and night. Their practical value to my congregation does not seem to me less than it was then. But they have been so incorporated into the very substance of my faith and life, that the intense intellectual interest which they once excited has gone by. I could not state them now with the same energy with which I stated them when they absorbed my whole thought and fired me with enthusiastic ardour. And yet when I take up an old sermon in which these aspects of truth or duty are illustrated and enforced, the flame bursts out again; I am ten, fifteen years younger; I can preach the sermon with the same vehement moral interest with which I preached it first. Sometimes, indeed, I think I preach an old sermon of this kind with even stronger emotion than I felt when it was fresh, for the experience of subsequent years has deepened my sense of the value of the truth or the sacredness of the duty which it was intended to illustrate. If, however, I had to write a new sermon on the same subject, I should not be able to write with the same force and fire.

You will be good enough not to misunderstand my meaning. I do not suggest that if you write and read, you should preach over again the sermons which strike you as very "pretty," or very "fine." The sermons which we have a right to repeat are sermons to which we have given so much time and strength that they contain the very best that we can say on some great subject; or sermons which, though of permanent interest and value, derived their force from the special intellectual and moral experiences which we were passing through when they were written.

When you preach an old sermon, be frank about it. There are people who keep a record of our sermons; the margins of their Bibles are enriched with dates placed against the texts we have preached from. Do not try to cheat these keepers of homiletical chronicles. The old sermon may sometimes require a great deal of revision: you may have to cancel some passages and replace them with others; you may have to strike out many superfluous epithets, to improve the form of an illustration, to strengthen the foundations or change the structure of an argument; but do not try to conceal the fact that the sermon is not a new one; let the old text stand.

Do you say that if you preach old sermons and the people know it they will think that you are getting lazy? If there is any chance of your people thinking that you are lazy, you have no right to preach at all. A man who is doing his work as he ought to do it, will be quite safe from imputations of that sort.

There is something to be said, then, in favour of writing our sermons and reading them; and there is something still more decisive to be said for the practice than I have said yet. It is certain that there are many able and useful preachers, who, if they did not use their manuscript, would be unable to preach at all.

And yet—notwithstanding my own habits—I am compelled to admit that if we can preach without reading we are likely to preach more effectively.

It is not true that read sermons are always dry and dull, or that extemporaneous sermons are necessarily vivacious and vigorous. Dr. Chalmers was accustomed to read every syllable, and yet he preached with a fire and a passion which created great excitement and produced the deepest impression. How weak, how dreary, an extemporaneous preacher may be, we all know. But there are few of us that have Dr. Chalmers's strong and impetuous nature. Unless there is extraordinary force in the preacher, the manuscript somehow comes between him and the congregation. The very reasons which lead us to say that we cannot preach unless we read, suggest some of the causes which make written sermons ineffective. If a preacher reads because he is afraid that he cannot carry in his mind all the thought that he is accustomed to put into a sermon, the probability is that the thought is wanting in simplicity and breadth ; that it is not well massed ; that the details are so numerous as to be confusing; and that, as a natural and almost inevitable consequence, the congregation will master his meaning very imperfectly. Or if he is conscious that what he wishes to say is not quite familiar to himself, and that he must write, in order to make sure of expressing it clearly, he may infer that he is not in such complete possession of it as to be able to handle it—even in writing—with freedom and vigour. If the thought—

though perfectly familiar to the preacher—is so subtle and so delicate that a great deal of care is necessary to express it accurately, the presumption is that it is too subtle and delicate to be caught at a single hearing, no matter how felicitous the expression may be. The thought of an extemporaneous preacher is more likely to be of a kind to interest and impress an ordinary congregation than the thought of a preacher who reads.

In the development of his thought the extemporaneous preacher has an advantage to which it is hardly possible to attach too great importance. When we are writing, it is not easy to determine at what point we ought to stop in working out an idea. If the idea has life in it, and our fancy happens to be fertile, there is a great intellectual delight in letting a single thought shoot out branch after branch covered with foliage and blossom. For an Essay, in which the intellectual interest is supreme, there is no harm in permitting our fancy to have its way ; but in a sermon, in which the practical interest dominates everything else, restraint is necessary if we are to be effective. As soon as the people are conscious that we have been caught by the mere intellectual attractions of any thought that has occurred to us, they become either impatient or critical; they want us to pass on, or else they watch our performance with curious eyes, to see whether we get through it gracefully and brilliantly. The extemporaneous preacher—even though he may have prepared the substance of a passage that is too elaborately ingenious—is checked by the direct relations between himself and his audience. He might have read it without being conscious that he was at fault; but, if he has any oratorical instinct, it is impossible for him to speak it.

The extemporaneous preacher will also be likely to have an advantage in his style. It is true that he can hardly be accurate. I met a few years ago some very able parliamentary reporters, and they told me that there were only three or four men in the House of Commons whose speeches it was possible to report exactly as they were spoken. But what the extemporaneous speaker loses in accuracy, he may more than gain in ease, directness, and vigour. He will escape the formality and the "bookishness" of manner which are the snare of most writers, and which are intolerable to all listeners; and in the generous heat which comes from direct contact with his audience, he may achieve a boldness both of thought and expression which are rarely achieved at the desk.

There is another advantage which belongs to the extemporaneous speaker. In writing, we cannot be sure whether we ought to be satisfied with saying a thing once, or whether we ought to say it over again. In speaking extemporaneously, we watch the faces of the people, and we often discover that statements which seemed to ourselves perfectly clear, require to be repeated, illustrated, and expanded.

I admit that the question cannot be determined peremptorily; that there are advantages on the side of preaching from a full manuscript, as well as advantages on the side of preaching from the briefest notes, or from no notes at all. Very much depends on the preacher, very much on the character of the congregation. There are, too, some subjects which may be treated as effectively by the man who reads his sermons as by the man who preaches extemporaneously. But I say again that, on the whole, I am clear that the practice of reading our sermons lessens the interest and impairs the power of our preaching.

If you determine—as I trust you will—not to read, you will do well to master the materials you have prepared for a sermon in the same way in which men master the materials they have prepared for a speech. On a few sheets of note-paper—if you cannot trust your memory—you may indicate your leading lines of thought, and the illustrations which you are most anxious not to forget. You will find it expedient to prepare two or three opening sentences; it is still more expedient to make sure of an effective close. One of the best speakers I have ever heard was often in the greatest difficulty through his inability to hit upon a perfectly satisfactory sentence to finish with. Those of us who knew him used to watch him with the greatest amusement while he was hunting to the right and to the left for what he wanted. We used to say that he was "running after his tail." If you have an illustration which requires perfection of form, you may write it out carefully and commit it to memory. You may also prepare a few keen, epigrammatic, or passionate sentences, in which to concentrate the effect of extemporaneous passages which lead up to them. I believe that Plunket, one of the greatest of our orators, was accustomed to prepare his speeches in this way. It is generally understood that on great occasions Mr. Bright follows the same method.

You need not be afraid that the sentences and passages which you have prepared will look like Horace's "purple patches" on the meaner fabric of your extemporaneous style, or that they will at all embarrass the free play of thought and passion. There is great shrewdness in the criticism of George Sand on the vehement words in which one of her heroes—a law student—denounced the practice of law —"They came to him too naturally not to have been studied."[1] If you have the true instinct and habit of a speaker, these prepared passages will simply heighten the effect and complete the impression of the rest of your sermon.

As for the extemporaneous passages, let them be perfectly extemporaneous. Make no attempt to recall the words in which your thoughts occurred to you in your study. Never permit yourself to criticise the form of your sentences; grasp your thoughts firmly, and let the sentences take their chance. The advice of Mr. Pitt to Lord Mornington was admirable. "My lord," he said, "you are not so successful as you ought to be in the House of Commons, and the reason, as I conceive, is this: you are more anxious about words

[1] George Sand: "Horace," p. 11.

than about ideas. You do not consider that if you are thinking of words you will have no ideas, but if you have ideas words will come of themselves." Lord Mornington—who is better known as the Marquis of Wellesley—took Pitt's advice, and he became one of the most eloquent of English orators.

But though you ought not to think of your style while you are preaching, you must think of it at other times. Whether you read your sermons or preach extemporaneously, it is equally necessary that you should take a great deal of trouble to acquire a mastery of the English language. Do not imagine that a knowledge of your own tongue will come to you by instinct or inspiration. The power of writing and speaking in clear, strong, racy, picturesque, and musical English is as truly the result of culture and hard work as the power of reading a play of Æschylus or a difficult speech in Thucydides.

I trust that you are already acquiring a discriminating admiration for the characteristic qualities of the great writers of English prose. The pomp and splendour and vigour of Edmund Burke, the masculine strength of Robert South, the ease of Cowper, the perfect transparency and unrivalled felicity of Archdeacon Paley, the subtlety and flexibility of Nathanael Hawthorne—you are learning, I hope, to find delight in them all. But mere delight is not enough. Voltaire used to keep the "Petit Carême" of Massillon always on his table. Dr. Johnson, oddly enough, considering his own ponderous and artificial manner, said that whoever would write English must spend his days and nights in the study of Addison.

You will not, if you are wise, try to imitate the style of any of the men whom you admire. "A man who writes well," says Montesquieu, "does not write as other men write; he writes in his own way;" and he adds, with a Frenchman's delight in an epigram, "he often speaks well when he speaks badly."[1] A man's style if it is a good one fits his thought like a good coat fits his figure. Your friend's coat may fit him admirably; but everything depends upon the fall of his shoulders, the length of his arms, and the breadth of his chest. If you tried to wear it you might find that you had put on a strait-jacket, or that the garment which, when worn by your friend, was perfectly graceful, hung about you like a sack.

Do not imitate the style of the great writers, but study them closely enough to learn how infinitely varied are the resources of the English tongue. You will find it, I think, a useful practice, after reading a paragraph which seems to you to be expressed with unusual clearness and force, to lay aside the book and to endeavour to express the same thoughts yourself. To compare your own handiwork with the bright original will be an instructive exercise: I have found it a very humiliating one. As you read, you may enlarge your vocabulary by marking and remembering words—not rare and remarkable words—but very ordinary and useful words, which never place themselves at the service of your thought.

[1] Montesquieu: "Pensées Diverses," p. 226.

You will notice idiomatic phrases and forms of sentences which you never employ. You will discover the various styles of architecture which may be followed in the building up of paragraphs — styles as different as Gothic and Grecian, Egyptian and Lombardic. One man begins by stating the general principle which the paragraph is to illustrate in detail. Another puts his concrete illustrations first, and the general principle explodes epigrammatically in the sentence with which the paragraph closes. Another ascends through details to a general principle, and then descends to details again.

The "theme" of a paragraph may, of course, be something very different from a general principle. The observations I have just made are intended simply to show what I mean by the different forms which a paragraph may assume.

Nor is it the great prose writers alone who will assist you in writing and speaking good English. For the language of pathos and humour, imagination and fancy, you will also study the poets—the poets who have won their place among English classics.

Men who have to preach twice every Sunday, and most of whose week evenings during eight months in the year are spent in lecturing, preaching, speaking, or conducting Bible-classes, cannot hope to acquire a very noble or beautiful style. But there is no reason why our sentences should all be run into one mould ; or why we should lose ourselves every few minutes in the mazes of an unintelligible parenthesis, or why our sermons should be like those of a preacher it was my happiness to hear occasionally when I was your age, each of which invariably consisted of one unwieldy sentence, sprouting out into joint after joint, and never ceasing to grow till for some inexplicable but beneficent reason the preacher said Amen. There is no reason why, when you have at your service the noblest language for an orator that was ever spoken by the human race, you should be satisfied with the threadbare phrases, the tawdry tarnished finery, the patched and ragged garments with a smell like that of the stock of a second-hand clothes shop, with which half-educated and ambitious declaimers are content to cover the nakedness of their thoughts. You can do something better than this, and you should resolve to do it.

Perhaps the most difficult of all styles to acquire is a style perfectly appropriate to public prayer. The mere language of our prayers may seem to some of you comparatively unimportant, but I think that not only intelligent and cultivated men, but very ordinary people, are sensitive to the qualities which render a style suitable to the purposes of devotion. They may find it impossible to explain why it is that when they are listening to one man's prayers their hearts are filled with awe and reverence and devout trust, and that when they are listening to the prayers of another man, who is not less devout, they find it almost impossible to pray at all; but the difference in the mere style of the prayers may often suggest a partial explanation of the difficulty. Phrases which when they were fresh were very beautiful, but from which the delicate bloom has long ago been quite rubbed off; heterogeneous fragments of ill-remembered and ill-applied sentences from the Psalms of David, the prophecies of Isaiah, and the hymns of Dr. Watts and Charles Wesley—these, to a man who is offering prayer, may seem to express his own devotional feeling, but they do not really express it, and they make it very difficult for many who are listening to him to maintain a devotional temper. The language of conversational familiarity is worse still. Rhetorical finery is most offensive of all.

These are gross faults easily avoided. No devout man of any education need pray in a style which will hinder the devotion of others. To acquire the natural use of a style which shall assist the devotion of those who listen to us, just as the music of a penitential hymn breathes a deeper pathos into its confessions of weakness and sin, and just as the music of a hymn of thanksgiving adds new passion to its gratitude, is not so easy.

That there should be a difference between the language of prayer and the language of preaching ought to occasion no greater perplexity than the very obvious fact that there should be a difference between the language of a sermon and the language of a hymn. Wordsworth, as you remember, contended that the style of a poem becomes unnatural just in the degree in which it varies from good prose. The theory

—happily it was a theory which he rarely practised—is at once destroyed by a comparison between any page of Wordsworth's prose and any page of Wordsworth's sonnets. It would be as rational to affirm that singing becomes unnatural just in the degree in which it varies from ordinary speaking. Every word that may be used by a poet may, perhaps, sometimes be used by a good prose writer; nearly every form of construction that is admissible in verse is admissible in certain kinds of prose; but there are words, there are turns of expression, there are phrases, which are perfectly in their place in the columns of a newspaper or in the pages of a review, which no poet would dream of using in serious verse. It seems to me that there are similar limitations—limitations still more subtle perhaps—which have to be recognised in our prayers, and which should distinguish the style of our prayers from the style of our preaching. I cannot define the difference between the two styles. The critics who rightly controverted Wordsworth's theory found it difficult to define the difference between the style appropriate to verse and the style appropriate to prose. But in both cases the difference exists.

A friend of mine, whose prayers were perfect in the simplicity and beauty of their form, told me that he thought no word should be used in prayer that had come into the language since the time of Queen Elizabeth. The canon seemed to me artificial, and most of us would find great difficulty in observing it; but in his own case it was certainly used with admirable results. The reasons for using in prayer old words which are still living words, will be obvious to every one that has thought about the philosophy of language. Perhaps, instead of adopting my friend's rule, it might be well to determine to use in prayer those words only which are found in our authorized version of the Bible, and to attempt, in the form of our sentences, the utmost simplicity of syntactical structure.

Before closing this lecture I should like to say something about those vices of style to which young writers and speakers are especially liable. But I am conscious of the same difficulty which troubled me in the early part of the lecture, in which I recommended you to preach extemporaneously. The precepts which I most honour I have found it hardest to obey. The faults which seem to me most serious are those which I have always found it difficult to avoid.

Perhaps I shall be less vividly conscious of my inconsistency — and I shall certainly speak to better purpose—if I invoke the authority of two or three great French writers instead of using my own words.

Montesquieu reminds us that the easiest style of all is the inflated and emphatic style; but this, he says, is the style of a nation just emerging from barbarism.[1] Joubert has several maxims in which he insists on the great virtue of simplicity. "Words, like lenses, obscure what they do not enable us to see better."[2] "The

[1] Montesquieu : " Pensées Diverses," p. 233.
[2] Joubert : " Pensées, Essais, et Maximes," vol. ii. p. 61.

oratorical style has often the disadvantage of those operas in which the music prevents the words from being heard : in this case, the words prevent you from seeing the thoughts."[1] Vauvenargues asserts that if a thought cannot be expressed in simple words, it is not worth expressing at all. " When a thought is not strong enough to bear a simple expression, that is a reason for rejecting it."[2] Joubert has also a maxim which suggests the necessity of varying our style according to the quality and power of our voice, and according to the size as well as the character of our congregation.[3] A tenor song, even though you transpose it a fifth lower, will not suit a bass singer ; and the style of speaking which may be very effective for a man with a shrill, keen voice, may be absolutely grotesque if attempted by a man whose voice is rich and deep and full. Some of the lady orators whom I have heard do not seem to have thought of this. They speak like men. It is just as if you played on the flute a piece of music written for the bass viol. The ladies must hit upon a new style of eloquence if they intend to be effective public speakers. One or two lady orators, whose originality of intellectual power and strong individuality save them from being imitators, seem to be striking the right path, but they have a long way to travel.

There are two other maxims of Joubert's which are

[1] Joubert : " Pensées, Essais, et Maximes," vol. ii. p. 80.
[2] Vauvenargues : " Réflexions et Maximes," p. 1.
[3] Joubert. Vol. ii. p. 61.

worth thinking of every day. "It is by familiar words that a style bites and takes possession of the reader. It is by these that great thoughts obtain currency and are assumed to be good metal, like gold and silver stamped with a well-known impression."[1] Again: "It is not enough to make people understand what you say; you must make them see it. The memory, the understanding, and the imagination must all take possession of it."[2] In another maxim he passes out of the region of literary criticism and touches the region of morals. "Let your mind always be loftier than your thoughts, and your thoughts loftier than your language."[3] If this maxim needs a commentary, you have it in the well-known verses by John Henry Newman, in the "Lyra Apostolica."

> "Prune thou thy words, the thoughts control,
>   That o'er thee swell and throng;
> They will condense within thy soul,
>   And change to purpose strong.
>
> "But he who lets his feelings run
>   In soft, luxurious flow,
> Shrinks when hard service must be done,
>   And faints at every woe.
>
> "Faith's meanest deed more favour bears,
>   Where hearts and wills are weighed,
> Than brightest transports, choicest prayers,
>   Which bloom their hour and fade."[3]

"By thy words thou shalt be justified, and by thy words thou shalt be condemned." This warning of our

---

[1] Joubert. Vol. ii. p. 81.   [2] Ibid.   [3] Ibid. 68.
[3] "Lyra Apostolica," p. 85.

Lord's has a special meaning for us ministers. The morality of a merchant consists very largely in the way in which he deals with money; the morality of a minister consists very largely in the way in which he deals with thoughts and words. There is an integrity of the intellect as well as of the exchange. We are not honest, merely because our words agree with our thoughts; honesty requires that we should do our best to make our thoughts agree with the facts. And for truthfulness of speech, it is not enough that we never say what we know to be false; we must do our best to form a style that shall be an accurate expression of our inner thought and life.

The morality of style is a subject so interesting that I wonder it has never been discussed. Some one said that Gibbon's style was a style in which it was impossible to speak the truth. There are other vices with which a style may be chargeable besides untruthfulness. Young ladies display their vanity in their dress and jewels, and perhaps they are sometimes reproved by young preachers who display equal vanity in the glittering phrases with which they bedizen their sermons—phrases which they want you to admire as much as if they were diamonds, but which are mere paste set in base metal. A style with magnificent qualities may sometimes touch the line which separates great excellences from great vices. Lord Macaulay was conscious that his own style was very near being a bad one. It may be doubted whether he altogether escaped the perils of which his strong clear sense warned him. But there can be no doubt that in the hands of his imitators his style has become as bad as a style can be—ostentatious, domineering, and tyrannical. Lord Macaulay's manner is very contagious. The miserable fate of those who have imitated him should teach us to avoid it.

Some young speakers and writers seem to be greatly fascinated with a style which has become common in some of our cheaper English newspapers during the last few years, and which I have occasionally met with in sermons published on both sides of the Atlantic. I do not know how to describe it except by calling it "the hot gin-and-water style"—the gin greatly predominating over the water. Sometimes it becomes maudlin, sometimes hysterical. It is the style of men who are guilty, intellectually, of an habitual violation of the laws of temperance and sobriety. I suppose that there was an original want of firmness in the fibre of their intellectual nature, and as the result of their love of intellectual excitement, and their impatience of plain honest work, they have become permanently diseased. Their intellectual condition reminds one of what the doctors say about men who have drunk so constantly and so heavily, that their blood and brain are alcoholised. These unfortunate writers may never touch a stimulant, but they suffer from intellectual *delirium tremens.*

There is hardly a vice, there is hardly a virtue of moral conduct, that has not its correlative in style. Conceit, vanity and ambition, insolence and pride, selfishness, cowardice, slovenliness and indolence, intemperance and violence, pretentiousness and indifference to truth—you may find them all in style as well as in character. You may also find the opposite virtues — courage, frankness and honesty, humility, modesty and simplicity, sobriety, gentleness and industry. I do not mean that the vices of a man's style are always present in what we call his moral character. It sometimes happens that through accidents of temperament, or through defective early moral discipline, or through the imperfect development of conscience, ethical laws are grossly violated by the intellect which are rigorously respected in conduct.

Let me remind you, gentlemen, in conclusion, that your language is one of the noblest and most precious parts of that magnificent inheritance which you have received from a great ancestry. It is the living and glorious monument of the thought, the endurance, the achievements, and the sorrows of many generations. It has been created by the affections and by the toil of the common people, by the genius of orators and poets, by the speculations of philosophers, by the devotion of saints. It is a legacy from your remote forefathers in German forests whose virtues are celebrated by the severest of Roman historians. It preserves some of the most costly treasures of ancient civilisations. It is the fruit of long years of patient industry, of cruel wars, of voyages in strange seas, and of travels in strange lands. It is yours, but all the citizens of this great commonwealth have a property in it. It is yours, but we, too, who live on the other side of the ocean have rights in it which you are bound to respect. It is yours, but it is entailed on your children and your children's children, and you will do them a great wrong unless you transmit it to the next generation with its wealth unimpoverished and its dignity unimpaired.

You have no more right to injure the national language than to chip a statue or to run a penknife through a picture, in the national museum. To use words so loosely and inaccurately that their definite meaning is lost, is to commit an intellectual offence, corresponding to that of removing the landmarks of an ancient estate. To prostrate noble words to base uses is as great a wrong to the community as to deface a noble public monument. A word once degraded can rarely be restored to its original rank; the bloom once rubbed off by rude and unmannerly hands can rarely be recovered; when once defiled by gross and vulgar associations, its delicate purity is lost for ever.

Your language is not yours—not yours alone; it belongs to your country and to posterity. Take care that, so far as you are concerned, none of its fertile provinces are permitted to sink out of cultivation; take care that the cold grey sea is not permitted to encroach on the coast. Maintain its ancient idiom. Honour the laws which have governed its structure. While a language lives it must grow. Old words must gradually fall off from it, like dead leaves from a tree in autumn ; new words must express the new life, like the fresh leaves on a tree in spring. But if you are not the last to use the old words, do not be the first to use the new. A language lives on the lips of the people, not in the dictionary. A dictionary is not merely a home for living words ; it is a hospital for the sick ; it is a cemetery for the dead. We, who have the ear of the people, can help to keep the best part of the language alive. Let us resolve that we will do nothing to make Shakespeare and Spenser, and Milton and Dryden, and Hooker and Howe, and Barrow and Baxter, and Defoe and Addison, and Bolingbroke and Swift and Burke, less intelligible to posterity than they are to ourselves.

It is said of a distinguished German philosopher that he pursued his philosophical studies undisturbed and apparently uninterested by the supreme struggle of his country with Napoleon ; that "his patriotism was limited to the German language, whose powerful beauties he appreciated so keenly that it maddened him to see it wielded in the clumsy grasp of ordinary writers." [1] I cannot recommend you to cherish so exclusive a devotion to the language of your country that you shall become indifferent to the violation of its territory ; but among the duties which an educated American citizen owes to the Republic, this seems to me to have no inconsiderable place — the duty of maintaining the purity and the strength and the honour of the national tongue.

[1] Schopenhauer. See his Life, p. 47.

LECTURE VII.

EVANGELISTIC PREACHING.

GENTLEMEN,—In a volume of Essays on the Christian Ministry,[1] which I remember reading when I was a student—Essays, by the way, selected from your own *Biblical Repository* and other American periodicals—there was an anonymous paper, in which it was argued that a preacher ought to have a large and deep acquaintance with the life of the age in which he lives. "*A Knowledge of his own Times important to a Christian Minister*"—this was the title of the paper, and this was the proposition which the writer maintained with great earnestness, ingenuity, and eloquence. I wish he had written a second paper with a slightly different title—"*A Knowledge of* other Times than his own *important to a Christian Minister.*" For, not to mention many other topics which might have found a place in the second essay, the writer might have shown that the despondency—I might almost say the terror and despair — with which some good men speak of the forces which are hostile to the Christian Faith in our own days, would give place to

---

[1] "Essays on the Christian Ministry." Edited by W. H. Murch, D.D. London. Third edition. 1848.

hopefulness and courage if they knew more of the irreligion and unbelief of past centuries.

There is no reason, gentlemen, why in these times a Christian preacher need be out of heart, whether he preaches in America or in England.

Do you remind me of the passionate eagerness for wealth, which is one of the chief vices both of your country and of mine?—of the fierceness of commercial competition, which forces upon merchants, manufacturers, and tradesmen, who would be satisfied with a modest income, incessant vigilance and incessant labour in order to escape commercial ruin? Or are you dismayed by what you hear or what you see of the feverish restlessness which makes men incapable of living a quiet life, and which makes them crave incessantly for exciting and sensational pleasures?

But the men and women about you are, after all, God's children, and as He has not forgotten *them*, they are unable to forget Him. Like their fathers, they, too, are sometimes conscious of vague and mysterious yearnings for an unknown and infinite good. They, too, sometimes come into the shadow of vast and solemn thoughts about the life beyond the grave. To them, too, conscience reveals the august authority of the Eternal Law of Righteousness. They spend lonely hours in sick chambers. They watch by the bed of the dying. They mourn for their dead. The deeper sorrows, the deeper joys of human life, do not vary much from age to age. The fairest hopes still fall away like spring-blossoms, and the sweetest pleasures pass away like summer flowers; the strongest self-confidence is humiliated, the most vigorous ambition is thwarted. The old story is translated into new languages, but the plot remains the same.

In brain and muscle, in heart and lungs, in form and limb, men are very much the same to-day that they were centuries ago—in the times of great religious revivals, in the times of the apostles and of the Lord Jesus Christ Himself. The eyes of men are still open to the brightness of the heavens, and their ears to the sound of the wind. And so the avenues by which in past generations God found His way into the innermost depths of their moral and spiritual life are still unclosed. Men may still be penetrated with awe by the Divine righteousness, may still be touched by the Divine pity, may still be compelled to tremble by the fear of the Divine anger: they may still be made to long for the sound of God's voice, for the grasp of His hand, and for the vision of His glory.

As for the intellectual activity of our times, of which some good men are so afraid, I cannot see that there is anything in it to create alarm. There are grave perils, no doubt, in the moral tendency of certain philosophical theories, which shelter themselves under the authority of recent scientific speculations; but ever since St. Paul wrote to the Colossian Christians about that false Gnosis which was attracting them from the simplicity of the gospel, the Church has had to maintain a perpetual struggle against theories of human nature and of the universe, which threatened the very foundations of faith. It is one thing, however, to say that the ancient conflict between the truth of Christ and human unbelief is not yet over; it is another thing to be alarmed on account of the intellectual activity of our times. Intellectual activity is unhappily far less common than one would suppose, from the accounts which are sometimes given of it.

I do not find that the majority of the English people spend their days and nights in studying physical science, or that there is a universal and consuming passion for the writings of Mr. Herbert Spencer. Nor do I find that there is such an enthusiastic devotion to literature and art, that it is impossible to induce people to think of anything else. It is not true, so far as I know, that balls and garden-parties have had to be given up, because all the young ladies between sixteen and five and twenty are absorbed in the music of Herr Wagner or in the philosophy of Schopenhauer. It is not true, so far as I know, that cotton-manufacturers, iron-masters, merchants, farmers, have given up their newspapers, that they may have more leisure for making out the meaning of Mr. Robert Browning's later poems. Nor did I hear that the London Stock Exchange was closed last season while the Grosvenor Gallery was open, because the brokers were anxious to give all their time to the study of the remarkable paintings of Mr. Burne-Jones, and the Nocturnes in Blue and Silver, and the Harmonies in Amber and Black, of Mr. James Whistler. I can only speak for the people of London and Liverpool and Manchester and Birmingham, and for those I happen to know in some of the quieter towns and villages of the old country. In Boston and New York, in Chicago and Charlestown, among your western settlers and the farmers of New England, it may of course be altogether different.

Even among the men who are eminent for their scientific or literary attainments, it does not seem to me that, except in rare instances, science or literature so completely fills up the whole capacity of their thought, and obtains so complete a mastery of their passions, that they are incapable of being interested in ordinary affairs. I know literary men and scientific men who care for national politics and for municipal business. They even think about how they can get 5 per cent. for their investments instead of 4½; they go out to dinner like other people, and they can talk about the weather; they fall in love; they marry; they have a taste for old china and for furniture of the time of Queen Anne. Their knowledge brings them some noble excitements and satisfactions; but human nature in *them* is after all very much what it is in the rest of the race. They, too, are the children of God, and they have wants and capacities which neither science nor literature can ever satisfy.

The Christian Faith has lived through epochs of intellectual excitement at least as intense as that by which the more active intellectual life of our own day is exalted. Have you forgotten the enthusiasm and pride of the intellectual revival which came to Europe in the fourteenth and the fifteenth centuries? All the intellectual glory of ancient Greece suddenly flooded the mind of Italy, France, and Germany. The noblest eloquence, philosophy, poetry, and art which the world had ever known, and which had been almost forgotten for centuries, were restored to the scholars of Europe, and produced an intellectual intoxication which perhaps has hardly ever been equalled since. Men felt that never before had they seen the transcendent splendours of human genius—that never before had they even suspected the vast possibilities of the intellectual powers of man;—but that time of intellectual triumph was followed, not by the destruction of Faith, but by the greatest of all religious revivals in the history of the Christian Church, the Protestant Reformation.

The new learning of the Renaissance might naturally have been regarded with terror. Paganism was invested with an intellectual glory which for a time made the brightest triumphs of the intellect of Christendom look poor and dim. The new learning which came with these dazzling pretensions, dealt with many of the problems for which a solution had been sought in theology; and it appealed to those very elements of our nature which are stirred by religious faith. It was no wonder that for a time men listened to Plato and forgot St. Paul; that their imagination was filled by the solemn grandeur and the perfect beauty of the ancient tragedians, so that the eloquence of Isaiah and the pathos of the Psalms were for a time overborne.

The Science of our times is a less formidable rival

to Faith. It does not touch the great problems in which the heart of man is most deeply interested ; or, if it ventures to touch them, it ceases to be Science and becomes pure speculation.

It is of no avail to tell us about the structure of the lachrymal gland when we want to know how the sorrow which finds a momentary relief in tears is to receive a permanent consolation. In quiet times we can listen with keen and respectful interest to all that Science can tell us about our mysterious kinship to the inferior animals, and even to the lowest forms of vegetable life ; but there are times in which we are conscious of a kinship of another kind—kinship to a life that is above us as well as to a life that is below us—and the higher kinship provokes an intenser interest, and is felt to be our supreme concern. The laws of heat and light, the history of the physical universe, the structure of our own physical nature, provoke intellectual curiosity ; but the deeper passions of our hearts are not touched until we are spoken to about the origin, and obligation, and transcendent nobleness and beauty of that idea of goodness which haunts us and which we cannot reach ; about the struggles and triumphs of heroic virtue and the perfection of saints ; about the consciousness of fault and failure which clings to us and which we cannot throw off; about the possibility of a future existence, in which our baffled hopes of resolving into a perfect harmony the harsh discords of our moral life may be fulfilled ; about the authority of God, about access to the Divine presence in this world, and about a day of judgment in the world to come.

Of all these things Science knows nothing. As soon as we enter into the sphere of moral freedom we ascend to heights which are beyond the wing and beyond even the vision of scientific speculation; for Science knows of no laws which are not uniformly obeyed, and in Morals we have to do with laws which we are free to obey or to transgress.

There is no reason, gentlemen, for being afraid that the splendid scientific triumphs of our time, triumphs in which every devout heart ought to rejoice, will stand in the way of our work. The whole region of human nature to which we appeal, Science leaves quite untouched.

Every age, however, has its superstitions, and one of the curious susperstitions of our own days may, perhaps, impair the energy of your own faith, and so diminish the force of your preaching. It seems to be taken for granted that because a man is very great on the life and structure of flowers and animals, he has exceptional authority on questions about God and immortality; and that because he knows a great deal about light and heat and electricity, he is sure to have very much to tell us about the spiritual universe. Yet no one supposes that because a man is a learned lawyer he is likely to give us safe advice about how to treat scarlet fever; and no one thinks that because a man is a very skilful physician, he has any claim to speak with authority on the best form of construction for steam-boilers or on the merits of a new plough. Even among scientific men themselves you will hear it said, Mr. —— is a great astronomer, but he knows nothing of biology; or he is a profound chemist, but he knows nothing of physiology. It is plain that a man may be eminent in one branch of physical science, and that in another branch his opinion may not be worth listening to: it is still more obvious that when a scientific man discusses ethical questions and questions of spiritual philosophy, he is dealing with subjects which are so remote from his usual studies, that his scientific knowledge and discipline give his opinions no claim to exceptional deference. To attach weight to a man's views on the authenticity of the four Gospels, or on any questions of religious truth and duty, because he is a distinguished geologist, chemist, or biologist, is just as preposterous as to attach weight to a man's views on geology because he is a profound theologian. The story of the conflict between Science and Religion is full of interest and of instruction, but it is only half finished. A century or two hence, when a few additional chapters will have to be written, some of our brilliant and eloquent contemporaries, who on scientific grounds—and with all the authority derived from their scientific achievements, are requiring us to abandon our faith in moral freedom and our hope of a life beyond the grave, will take their turn in the pillory—will be the objects of the same scorn and derision as the theologians who in the name of the Church, and on the authority of the

Book of Genesis and the Book of Psalms, imprisoned Galileo, condemned Kepler's laws as religious heresies, and made it a treason against God to believe that the earth revolves on its axis, and was created more than six thousand years ago.

You, I hope, will make it a matter of conscience to avoid the error committed by theologians in past ages, and committed in another form by some scientific men in our own times. As religious teachers, you have absolutely no authority over questions lying within the province of Science. At no point in the working out of any scientific problem have you—as religious teachers—any right to interfere. You have no right to ask for any consideration of the interests of religious faith in the settlement of any scientific controversy. The judges in your law courts would resent as an insult to their integrity any suggestion that they should put the slightest pressure upon the law in order to favour the interests of their personal friends or of their political party. You offer an equal insult to the integrity of scientific men when you betray any wish that in their scientific inquiries they should be influenced by the way in which it is supposed that their conclusions might affect the authority of Divine revelation. It is part of their religious duty to settle scientific questions on scientific grounds, and on scientific grounds only. For you to wish them to work under a bias, is the indication of a flaw in your intellectual honesty, and a decisive proof of a want of courage and firmness in your religious faith.

To what extent it is our duty to discuss in the pulpit modern speculations—partly scientific, partly philosophical—which are hostile to the Christian Faith, is a question which every man must determine for himself. You must determine it by considering your own resources and the character of your congregation.

If you touch controversies of this kind, you ought to be quite certain that you understand the theories which you are attacking, and that you have mastered the grounds on which they rest. You ought, also, to be quite sure that you can reply—not to the weakest—but to the strongest arguments by which they are supported. The serious beliefs of men ought to be discussed seriously and fairly. It is perfectly legitimate to illustrate the grotesque absurdity of a false speculation when we can prove it to be false; it is perfectly legitimate to kindle a generous indignation against an intellectual imposture if we have the knowledge and skill to unmask it; but to attempt to laugh our opponents out of court without meeting their case, and to make passion take the place of reason, are shameful offences against the laws of intellectual honour and equity. I trust that the ethics of theological controversy are better understood by us than they were by our fathers; but theological controversialists, like controversialists of other kinds, are always under a strong temptation to seek fair ends by foul means. We have no right to secure the condemnation of the basest criminals by menacing the jury and bribing the judge. I do not believe in Lynch law, even for the worst crimes. It is dangerous to try to cast out devils in the name of Beelzebub the prince of the devils. We shall never fight the battles of Heaven to any purpose with arms forged in hell. To attempt to destroy even the most pernicious error by reckless misrepresentation, by appeals to ignorance and blind passion, by weapons poisoned with slander, is to repeat the crime of the Jesuits, who are credited with sanctioning the assassination of heretical princes. If you touch controversy, be just, be generous, to your opponents.

But it is doubtful whether it is wise for most of us, especially in the earlier years of our ministry, to carry on any direct controversy with scientific and philosophical unbelief. Sermons on subjects of this kind should, in any case, be preached very seldom. In ordinary congregations there are very few persons who have any exact knowledge of the speculations by which the Christian Faith is menaced, very few who are acquainted with the scientific grounds on which most of these speculations rest, very few who are trained to those intellectual habits which are necessary for forming any intelligent judgment on them. Our true business—and this we should be careful not to neglect—is to secure our own territory. So far as Science is concerned, the war we have to carry on is purely defensive. In our case, the principle of non-interference is not only legitimate but obligatory. As theologians, we have no occasion to be troubled so long as our neighbours do not pass our frontier. We may leave it to scientific men to discuss the claims of Darwinianism on scientific allegiance ; to us as theologians the settlement of the scientific controversy has no practical interest. Our only interest is to know the truth. It is, perhaps, impossible for us to maintain an absolute neutrality of feeling while watching the civil strife which disturbs a neighbouring kingdom, and there are many reasons which might lead us to prefer that the struggle should be settled in favour of Mr. Darwin's theory rather than against it ; but we must respect the rights of belligerents while the struggle lasts, and we are prepared to accept whatever theory may ultimately make good its authority.

We are not prepared, however, to yield to either party an inch of the soil which belongs to ourselves, and which it is our duty to defend. A defensive controversy is imposed upon us as a necessity. In the name of Science, in the name of Philosophy, theories are propagated which undermine moral responsibility and train the soul, first to ignore and then to deny the existence and the authority of the living God. These theories are in the air. They determine the method of many social speculations which to innocent minds seem to have no relation to religious truth. They are the fundamental assumptions which underlie a great deal of historical criticism. They give a colour to leading articles on the political questions of the hour. You find them everywhere.

I believe that the wisest and most effective way of

dealing with these theories is to insist very earnestly on the moral and religious truths which are imperilled. The scientific speculations — true or false — are no special concern of ours. The moral and religious truths which are menaced have their own evidence. The issue of the controversy largely depends, for the moment, upon the vigour and authority of conscience, and upon the ardour and vehemence of those moral affections which are the allies of conscience and the strong defenders of her throne. Let there be a regular and systematic endeavour to strengthen among the members of your congregations the sense of moral responsibility. Give no quarter to the miserable and ignominious doctrine that the moral character of a man is determined by his environment. Heap up fires of indignation on the excuses that men find for their crimes in their circumstances. While frankly acknowledging that physical temperament, early education, the nature of a man's employment, his social position, his success or failure in business, the food he eats, the very temperature of the air he breathes, may affect his moral life injuriously or favourably, teach men that it is the prerogative of human nature to force and compel the most adverse circumstances to give new firmness to integrity and new fire to enthusiasm, to harden the fibre of courage, to make generosity more genial and pity more compassionate, to exalt innocence to virtue and virtue to heroism. The literature of all ages and all countries is on your side—history, poetry, and eloquence ; the common speech of all nations is on your side—language, which is the expression of the enduring instincts of human nature, refuses to confound crime and misfortune, affirms a distinction of infinite and eternal significance between the conditions of human life for which men are to be pitied or envied, and the moral acts for which they are to be honoured or condemned ; the conscience of every man to whom you speak is on your side, and though drugged by immoral sophistries, or almost driven from her throne by the revolt of evil passions, let her hear your voice asserting her regal titles, and calling back her subject powers to their allegiance, and she will spring up in terrible and glorious majesty—an archangel of God, armed with the lightnings and thunders of Heaven. Robust ethical preaching is one of the surest defences against the worst and most prevalent forms of modern unbelief.

A vigorous conscience is not only a protection against those materialistic theories of the universe which deny the reality of Moral Freedom, it is also the surest and most trustworthy ally of faith in the Living God. It is the moral side of human nature that touches the Divine. It is through the consciousness that we ourselves have a will which moves freely among natural laws, and is not bound by them, that we are able to believe in a God who is above Nature. Let the consciousness of Moral Freedom be lost or become feeble, and by no metaphysical searching will men be able to find out a personal God.

But if men are to be held fast to their religious

faith by the instincts of their moral life, the God we preach must not be a kindly good-natured God, who does not think very seriously of our moral character, who cares more for our comfort than for our righteousness, who commands no obedience, but leaves us to order our lives as we please, "according to our light," who threatens sin with no penalties, and will make us all happy at last. This sentimental conception of God corresponds to no reality. The relations between God and ourselves are wholly misconceived when we forget that He has a right to rule, and that we are under an obligation to obey. The conception is powerless as well as false. It never secures any firm hold of the deeper life of men. They part with it and are conscious of no loss; none of the great forces which stir human passion and inspire human energy are missed. We must assert God's authority; and if we assert it there are irrepressible instincts in the moral and spiritual life which will confess the duty of submission.

But should we not try to meet men on their own ground? It is just as true that God loves men as that He claims authority over them;—is it not our wisdom to present those aspects of truth which attract sympathy and provoke no antagonism? If we adopt any other line, shall we not destroy what little faith some men still retain? Every one will listen to us when we speak of the Divine love, but to the idea of God's moral authority, and especially to the idea that this authority will be resolutely maintained, the temper and spirit of our age are irreconcilable.

"Meet men on their own ground?" Yes. But the only legitimate reason for meeting them on their own ground is the intention to persuade them to come over to ours. We may "meet them on their own ground," but if we remain on the ground which is occupied by those who are in revolt against Christ, we go over to the camp of the enemy. Some preachers seem to suppose that the true method of converting unbelievers is to explain away or to conceal everything in the Christian faith to which unbelievers object, and to emphasise everything in it which they are willing to admit. While listening to preachers of this kind, men cannot help thinking that if there is so very little difference between what is contained in the gospel and what they have discovered for themselves, and so very little difference between what they are already and what they would have to become if they acknowledged the Christian law of life, their conversion to Christ must be a matter of very slight importance.

I believe that the principle which should govern the Christian preacher is precisely the reverse of that which is accepted by these pleasant and accommodating apologists. Addressing men who have an honourable abhorrence of untruthfulness and injustice, but who ignore the personal claims of Christ on their obedience and their trust, I should never hope to convert them by insisting that according to the teaching of Christ no reverence for Himself is of any worth apart from moral integrity; nor should I have any hope of converting charitable persons who are insensible to the claims of the Divine authority by expatiating on those parts of our Lord's teaching which urge the claims of human poverty and suffering. In England, and I suppose in America, there are large numbers of people who acknowledge the ethical beauty of our Lord's teaching and the ideal perfection of His character, but who cannot tolerate the awful menaces which He uttered against the impenitent, and who refuse to acknowledge that faith in Christ can be the condition of everlasting life, and that unbelief will end in everlasting destruction. Such persons will listen to us with perfect complacency while we discourse on the duty of gentleness, kindness, and self-sacrifice, and while we illustrate the infinite mercy and compassion of our Father in heaven. Preaching of this sort will not provoke their resentment; it will command their sympathy and admiration. But though everything that we say on these subjects may be true, we shall never, by preaching exclusively on subjects of this kind, overcome their deeply-rooted hostility to the authority of Christ. To preach to such persons in this way, and in this way only, is what I mean by meeting them on their own ground and remaining there.

But was not this St. Paul's policy at Athens? Did he not appeal to the inscription on a heathen altar, and found an argument on a quotation from a heathen poet? No doubt. But when he appealed to the inscription on one of their own altars, it was not with the intention of assuring them that they had already discovered nearly everything that he could tell them about the " God that made the world and all things therein : " the inscription is used with consummate grace to imply that though God created us, and is " not far from every one of us," and though " in him we live and move and have our being," to the Athenians He was " an unknown God." The line from an ancient poet is not quoted to show that the Greeks had already anticipated a large part of the revelation which it was St. Paul's commission to make known to mankind : it was quoted with the express object of attacking the whole system of idolatry : " Forasmuch, then, as we are the offspring of God, we ought not to think that the Godhead is like unto gold or silver or stone, graven by art and man's device." This was St. Paul's method of meeting unbelievers on their own ground. He found his way into their fortifications to turn their own guns upon them. He exploded their whole system from within. He quoted the inscription on one of their own altars in order to suggest that neither their philosophy nor the traditions of their ancestors had given them any knowledge of the true God. He quoted Aratus or Kleanthes in order to expose the ignorance of the Divine greatness which was illustrated by the temples and statues which they had erected in honour of their divinities.

Nor—though this was the first discourse that he delivered to them—did he keep within the limits of philosophical discussion about the nature of God, and the true method of worshipping Him. He went on at once to speak about judgment to come, and about Christ's resurrection from the dead. He might, had he chosen, have said many things to which the Epicureans and Stoics would have listened with interest, and even with respect. He might have discussed questions of morals. He might have compared or contrasted the ethical teaching of Christ with their own. But all this would have been to no purpose. The resurrection of Christ might provoke their mockery, but to be silent about it would have given them a false conception of the gospel. It was more important that the Athenians should know the truth—whether they received it or not—than that St. Paul should conciliate their respect.

The principle on which I am insisting is a very simple one: whether true or false, it is intelligible. We shall never make men Christians by suppressing and throwing into the shade those parts of the Christian revelation which especially provoke their hostility. Truth which men regard as incredible, truth which men resent—we must be sure, first of all, that it is truth, and truth of an important kind—is precisely the truth which men most need to hear, and which is likely to produce the deepest moral impression. In this age, therefore, when, according to the theory of some thinkers who are exerting a powerful influence over popular thought on both sides of the Atlantic, ethics and religion are little if anything more than a branch of physiology; when the worst passions of bad men and the devotion of saints are regarded as mere functions of our physical organisation; when vice and virtue are supposed to be "products like sugar and vitriol, the laws of whose production Science may be expected to discover;" when the will is treated as only one form of that universal force which, in whatever form it is revealed, is subject to fixed and invariable laws; when we are asked in the name of Science, and in the name of an unselfish devotion to humanity, to renounce the hope and even the desire of personal immortality, and to be satisfied if, by the labour and virtue of this transient life, we contribute something to the moral and intellectual development of the race; when we are asked to reduce our faith in God Himself to a belief in the omnipresence of something which passes comprehension, or at best are permitted to acknowledge Him as a power without us, that works for righteousness, a power that cannot be touched to pity by our sorrows, cannot be indignant when we sin, cannot watch with ardent sympathy our struggles with temptation, cannot rejoice with us in our triumphs and be troubled with us in our defeats;— in these days it is the duty of the Christian preacher to assert with greater energy than ever the moral freedom of man, the certainty of a life beyond the grave, and the personality and authority of the Living God.

Sermons on these elementary topics are not to be regarded as merely controversial, philosophical, or ethical. Their intention is to strengthen those natural instincts, and those elements of what may be called the natural faith of men, which are threatened by prevalent forms of unbelief, and to which the supernatural revelation which has come to us through Christ appeals. They should be penetrated with an evangelistic spirit, and their immediate or ultimate object should be to make men conscious of sin, and to prevail upon them to serve God.

Our evangelistic preaching might, perhaps, be more successful if we gave more careful and intelligent thought to the conditions of success. To tell men over and over again that they ought to repent and believe the gospel, to entreat them, no matter with what vehemence, to "accept Christ," will rarely produce any real results. Nor shall we do much by telling men that they ought to be afraid of God's anger, and that they ought to trust in His love. We have to present to their minds and hearts those truths which will make them wonder at the infinite greatness of the love of God, and which will make them afraid to provoke His wrath; those truths which will create repentance and inspire faith. I know that to preach the gospel so as to reach the hearts and consciences of men, we need a special gift of the Holy Ghost: this gift we ought to seek in earnest prayer. I know, too, that the preaching of even an apostle will be powerless apart from the direct action of the Spirit of God upon the souls of men; and the manifestation of the presence and power of the Spirit is not to be expected unless we pray for it. It remains true that the substance and manner of our preaching should be determined by the effect which we wish to produce.

I doubt whether we sufficiently consider the variety of motives which bring men to Christ, or the kind of preaching which is likely to call these motives into vigorous and effective action. There is room for a treatise on the Philosophy of Conversion, in which questions of this order might be investigated. In the absence of any such treatise, which if it were written by a competent hand would be invaluable, we must do the best we can for ourselves. Your remembrance of your own religious history and your knowledge of the religious history of your friends will furnish many suggestions that may be of use to you. These materials will be rapidly increased if you watch the religious life of the members of your congregations.

Some men begin to live a Christian life under a sense of duty. There is no keen sorrow for sin; there is no serious dread of the Divine anger; there is no fear of eternal perdition. Very much that usually precedes conversion follows it, and follows it sometimes after a long interval. Christ appeals to the conscience, and He is obeyed. There may be persons to whom we are preaching who will respond to this appeal, and to this appeal only. We should therefore ask how we can present the Christian life so as to compel the consciences of these men to confess that this is the kind of life they ought to live. We should consider how we can preach upon the moral greatness and authority of

Christ so as to make them feel that disloyalty to Him is a grave moral offence, and that to acknowledge Him as the Lord and Ruler of their lives is their supreme duty.

Other men are drawn to God by the hope of escaping from a vague dissatisfaction with themselves and with the poverty of their life. Young people soon find that life is not so large and rich and animating as they hoped it would be. In the absence of ambition, or of an exceptional enthusiasm for literature, science, or politics, or of the distraction produced by a rapid succession of stimulating pleasures, or of the nobler and more generous excitement which springs from happy love, there is something wanting; they know not what. There seems to be nothing worth living for. They are capable of an enthusiasm which there is nothing to excite, of a love and devotion which there is nothing to command. At such times, if they catch any glimpse of the wealth and fulness of the life which is possible to them through Christ, they may be won for ever. They may be won if they can be brought under the power of any of the grander aspects of the Christian revelation, if their hearts can be thrilled by its immortal hopes, if they can be stirred with the passionate devotion inspired by Christ's infinite love. Such persons may be reached by the appeal of the gospel to the moral imagination of man and to his deeper moral emotions.

In others there is something to which we can appeal that is more definite than this vague restlessness.

The native instincts of their spiritual life are no longer latent, and there is a keen solicitude to find God. They have half learned the open secret of Nature. They know what Wordsworth meant when he said:—

> "And I have felt
> A presence that disturbs me with the joy
> Of elevated thoughts; a sense sublime
> Of something far more deeply interfused,
> Whose dwelling is the light of setting suns,
> And the round ocean, and the living air,
> And the blue sky, and in the mind of man;
> A motion and a spirit that impels
> All thinking things, all objects of all thought,
> And rolls through all things."

Such men are sometimes idealists in philosophy, and read the transcendental poets. But they are conscious that the mysterious Presence escapes them. They know that the kingdom of heaven is near to them, and are striving to enter in, but somehow they are unable. They have to be taught the mystery of the new birth. To the pardon of sin and to justification they are as yet indifferent, but they will listen to the words of St. John about the eternal life which was with the Father and was manifested in Christ. They will listen to Christ when He speaks of Himself as the Way to the Father and as the true Vine, of which those who believe in Him are the branches. They may be reached by the mysticism of the gospel.

There are some, again, who begin to think of God through the shame and self-disgust which are the result of moral failure and the discovery of moral weakness. Their firmest resolutions are broken almost as soon as they are made. They fall under the power of the poorest and most ignoble temptations. They repent, and fall again. They become alarmed about themselves. There is no sense of sin, but there is an agony of moral shame, and sometimes they sink into moral despair. The gospel which will attract their hearts is the assurance that Christ can break the force of evil habits and destroy evil passions, and give them strength for all moral duty. This gospel they may receive before they discover clearly that what conscience condemns as vicious God condemns as sinful; but if they walk in the light which comes to them, no matter how faint the light may be, it will brighten into perfect day.

Other men, whose moral life is generous and aspiring, may approach Christ through those ethical precepts of His which require a perfection that is altogether impossible apart from the power of the Holy Spirit. They have been haunted by thoughts of an ideal and romantic goodness; but Christ's ethical precepts and His own character create still fairer and loftier visions of what human life might be. When they learn that the laws of Christ are promises in another form, and that the character of Christ is the prophecy of the perfection which is possible to those who receive the life of Christ, their moral enthusiasm will be kindled. They have very much to learn before they can receive the kingdom of heaven as little children; but if they are in earnest, the humility of faith will come at last.

There are many who are drawn to Christ by His love—drawn to Him, not because they are conscious either of moral weakness which His love is eager to strengthen, or of sin which His love is willing to forgive, or of unintelligible cravings which His love is able to satisfy—but by the love itself. They are drawn to Him as if by the force of moral and spiritual gravitation. Children, especially—if I may judge from my own observation—are drawn to Christ in this way. Whether the opinion is sound which is held by very many persons just now, that in nearly all cases it is the love of Christ that originates religious thought and 'life, seems to me very doubtful. That the opinion should be a common one, is explicable; for whatever may have first awakened religious earnestness, there must be an apprehension of the love of Christ before it is possible to have faith in Him; but this is no proof that the truths and facts which created the religious solicitude were superfluous. And yet it is certain that if we could preach about the love of Christ with the ardour, the exultation, and the rapture which it ought to inspire, there would be something contagious in our faith and joy; if we could preach about it with a tenderness like that which He Himself manifested to the weak and the sorrowful and the sinful, the hearts of men would be melted by it.

To preach with any effectiveness on Christ's love we ourselves must be full of the spirit of Christ, and we must have a vivid sense of the continuity of Christ's life. We must feel, and must make others feel, that we have not merely a history to tell, but that the Christ of the Gospels is alive ; that He has been living through all the centuries which separate our own age from the days in which men saw His human face and heard His human voice, and that He is living still ; that He does not merely reign on some golden throne in some remote world, surrounded by shining angels and by saints who have fought the good fight and received their crown, but that He is still seeking and saving the lost ; that in His heavenly glory He has lost none of the compassion and gentleness which win our affection in the story of His earthly humiliation ; that the men who were His contemporaries were no dearer to Him than the men of later generations; that He is still the very Christ who took the little children in His arms and blessed them; who saw the desolation of the poor widow at Nain as she and her friends were carrying her only son to the sepulchre, and who, without being asked, stopped the sorrowful company and restored the young man to His mother ; who, when He was reproached for eating with publicans and sinners, defended Himself in the parable of the Prodigal Son ; who wept when He thought of the calamities which were coming upon the city that rejected Him; who endured for us and for our salvation the agony of Gethsemane, and the desertion and death of the cross.

"The cross"—this, according to the consent of all Churches, and of all the evangelistic traditions of Christendom, is the supreme power of the gospel; and the power of the cross is the power of the love of Christ. And yet, not of the love of Christ only. For the sufferings of Christ were not a mere dramatic display of love. "I delivered unto you first of all," said St. Paul, writing to the Corinthians, "that which I also received, how that Christ died *for our sins.*" This truth, according to the greatest evangelist among the apostles, was one of the chief things, the fundamental things, that he made known to those heathen people when he preached the gospel to them. It is not enough to tell men that Christ died because He loved them; the gospel of the death of Christ includes the fact that He died for their sins. Until men know what sin is—sin as distinguished from mere natural defects and infirmities, which they may attribute to their temperament and to the physical constitution which they have inherited from their parents;—sin as distinguished from mere deformity which offends their ideal of moral grace and beauty;—sin as distinguished from mere vice, which conscience condemns, and which, in the absence of any belief in the authority or even the existence of the Living God, conscience would continue to condemn;—until, I say, men know what sin is they can see no meaning in a large part of St. Paul's gospel of the death of Christ. Until they are troubled, ashamed, and alarmed by the consciousness of sin, they will listen to a large part of this gospel with moral indifference, or even with moral resentment.

It should therefore be one of the principal objects

of the Christian preacher to discover how he can awaken the sense of guilt. He must be careful to avoid all those representations of God which encourage men to think that God is indifferent to human sin. He must not suffer even the Law of Righteousness to come between the conscience and God, but must train men to the recognition of the Divine authority over human life. To assert the authority of an impersonal Law will not create the consciousness of sin. Righteousness is the discharge of those duties which we owe to persons;[1] unrighteousness is the neglect of those duties; and what has been called the "higher law" is the law which arises from the relations between the human race and the Personal God. The Christian preacher must also insist on the ethical view of human nature, utterly refusing to make any compromise with theories which dull the sense of human responsibility, never losing any legitimate opportunity of giving emphasis to the truth that all the dignity and shame, the romance and the heroism, the tragedy and the glory, of the life of nations and of individual men, have their origin in the mysterious prerogative of moral freedom.

Sometimes the sense of guilt may be awakened by a deliberate and persistent assault on a particular vice; sometimes by compelling the conscience to pronounce

---

[1] See "Christianity and Morality:" the Boyle Lectures for 1874 and 1875. By Henry Wace, M.A. London: Pickering. These lectures are, in my judgment, the most valuable contribution to English theological thought that has been made for many years.

judgment on the character of a life which may be free from vice, but in which the authority of God counts for nothing. Sometimes a vivid presentation of the ideal of saintliness will suddenly reveal to men the contrast between what they are and what they ought to be. Sometimes men will become sensible of their guilt in the light of the infinite love of God. Sometimes they will start back with terror and astonishment and bitter sorrow when they discover that it was for their sins that the Christ was forsaken of the Father, and died a cruel and shameful death. The death of Christ, which is the supreme revelation of the Divine love, is also the supreme revelation of human guilt.

What are we to say of that appeal to fear which is denounced with such scorn and vehemence by the Christianity that claims to be "liberal," and teaches us to bring our religious faith into harmony with the spirit of the nineteenth century? I think that we have to ask ourselves, first of all, whether those who continue in revolt against God, and who refuse to receive the Christian redemption, have anything to fear? One of the soundest and noblest elements of the intellectual temper of the nineteenth century is its respect for facts. The great lesson which scientific men have been trying to teach us is that we cannot make a universe out of our own heads. Of late, indeed, scientific men themselves seem to have sometimes forgotten their own lesson; and by a singular Nemesis, some daring scientific speculations on the origin and constitution of the universe have recently been sharply criticised by Dr. Bridges, one of the chief English representatives of orthodox Positivism—not of orthodox Christianity—on the ground that they violate the fundamental canons of scientific inquiry.[1] Those who describe themselves as "liberal" Christians seem to me to be open to criticism of a similar kind. We may resent the intrusion of scientific methods into the sphere of ethics and religion, but if moralists and theologians can learn nothing else from science, they should at least learn this—that facts should govern speculation, and that if speculation, however brilliant and charming, refuses in its pride to acknowledge their authority, the facts will always be strong enough to hold their own.

I ask again whether those who continue in revolt against God, and who persistently reject the Christian redemption, have anything to fear? Christ spoke of "the worm that dieth not, and the fire that is not quenched." He said that there will be "wailing and gnashing of teeth" when the wicked are severed from the just and cast into "the furnace of fire;" that the wicked and slothful servant will be driven into the darkness without, when the Lord of all returns to hold high festival in light and joy with those who have served Him loyally; that when He comes with His holy angels and sits on the throne of His glory, He will say to the unmerciful, "Depart from me ye cursed." St. Paul speaks of the "indignation and wrath, tribulation and anguish," which are to come upon

[1] See *Fortnightly Review* for June and July, 1877.

those who know the law of God and break it; and warns those that obey not the gospel of our Lord Jesus Christ, that they will be "punished with everlasting destruction." Had St. Paul any authority to declare that this awful doom menaces the impenitent? He who came to seek and to save the lost—was He sure of His own mind when He affirmed that when all nations are gathered before Him, He will separate them into two companies, and that He will pronounce a curse on those who are on His left hand, and command them to depart from His presence into everlasting fire? Is this His settled purpose? Will He carry it out—not shrinking from the awful penalties which He threatens to inflict upon those whom He condemns? All that we actually know about the future — all that we *know*, as distinguished from what we imagine, from what we infer, from what we hope—we learn from Him who has brought life and immortality to light through the gospel, and who has also declared that unimaginable woes are the destiny of the unsaved. Is Christ's testimony to be trusted? This is the first question which we have to solve.

About the precise measure and character and duration of the evils of which He speaks, you may be uncertain. To insist that the lost will be punished in material fires, is as irrational as to insist that the saved will dwell in a city paved with material gold. You may think that the language of Christ and His apostles suggests that although the doom of the condemned is irrevocable, their sufferings will end in the exhaustion of life and strength, and in a second death, from which there will be no resurrection. You may even think that possibly there is some reserve in the revelation of the eternal future, and that He who will first command the wicked to depart from Him, will afterwards seek them in the desolation to which His own word had banished them, and will strive, not without success, to bring them back to light and to God. You must interpret the teaching of Christ for yourselves, remembering only that you have to discover—not what His words may be made to mean,—but what they meant; but however you interpret it, does there not remain something very appalling for the impenitent to fear? And while this remains, is it not a ground on which you may rest some of the strongest and most effective arguments for renouncing sin, and submitting to the authority of God?

To rely exclusively, or even chiefly, on terror as an instrument of conversion, is no doubt a grave mistake; but if we shrink from speaking of the Divine anger which sin provokes, and of the Divine resolution to inflict upon the impenitent intolerable punishment, we suppress truths which on the lips of wiser, firmer— yes, and I will add, more merciful—preachers than ourselves, have not only agitated men with alarm, but have constrained them to appeal to Christ for deliverance, at once from sin and from eternal death. There is one caution which I will venture to suggest, and I will give it in the words of a man who on this subject has a right to be heard with exceptional respect.

Mr. Moody once said to me that "a preacher ought to have a very tender heart, to speak with any good effect about the condition of the lost."

It was not my intention to attempt a complete account of the various elements of man's moral and spiritual nature to which the gospel appeals; I merely wanted to illustrate what I meant when I said that in our evangelistic preaching we ought to study the conditions of success. It is not by the monotonous repetition of a solitary truth, or by putting an incessant strain on a solitary motive, that we shall convert all sorts of men. It is our duty to consider the manner in which the varied contents of the Christian revelation affect the varied powers and passions and susceptibilities of human nature. We ought to try, in turn, every possible access to the conscience and the heart.

In saying this, I have assumed that there is no rigid and uniform type to which the spiritual life in its origin and development should be compelled to conform. It cannot matter how a man comes to Christ, if only he comes. Any motive that brings men to Christ is a legitimate motive. Do not permit yourselves to be fettered in your preaching by the formal conception of an exact succession of experiences through which every one that forsakes sin and lives for God must necessarily pass. John Bunyan made Christian flee from the City of Destruction in great terror, and carrying a heavy burden. The poor pilgrim sunk deep in the Slough of Despond; was frightened almost out of his life under the awful rocks and flames of Mount Sinai; carried his dreadful load on his weary shoulders long after he had passed through the Wicket-gate, and even after he had been shown the wonders and mysteries of the Interpreter's House. But when Christiana and her children started on their pilgrimage, Christiana had very little terror, and the children had no terror at all. The boys cried before setting out, but it was only because they had not gone with their father, and now they wanted to follow him. Not one of them sunk into the Slough; not one of them had a load to carry; and neither the cliffs nor the fires of Sinai alarmed them. John Bunyan was much wiser than those good men who cannot believe that little children are in the right way at all unless they can tell the story of how for a time they were almost crushed with the sense of guilt, and only found peace at the sight of the cross.

The city of God has twelve gates: every one of them is a gate of pearl. What presumption it is to insist that unless men enter by a particular gate they cannot enter at all! Let them enter by the gate that is nearest to them. Nor should we insist that to reach the gate itself there is only one path. Some men find their way to it by the high road of duty; some through ravines of gloomy desolation and despair; some across pleasant meadows, bright with the sunlight of hope and musical with the song of birds. When once they are among the happy nations of the saved, inside the jasper walls, no one will challenge their right to a place in the holy city because they entered by the wrong gate, or approached the right gate by the wrong road.

If we are to have exceptional success in the conversion of men we must have that exceptional form of spiritual force which has been granted to some great evangelists. "To one is given by the Spirit the word of wisdom; to another the word of knowledge by the same Spirit; to another faith by the same Spirit; . . . to another prophecy;" to another an evangelistic power which seems almost irresistible. "All these worketh that one and the selfsame Spirit, dividing to every man severally as he will." In some cases this power seems to have come to a man at the very beginning of his own religious life; in others, after many years of patient and earnest Christian work, which had achieved no extraordinary success; in some cases it has rested upon a man for a time and has then been withdrawn.

I do not know that we have any right to believe that this exceptional gift is to be obtained by every one that seeks it. Nor do I think, therefore, that if we have sought it and not received it, we are bound to suppose that the cause lies in our own sin and unbelief. "For the body is not one member, but many. . . . If the whole body were an eye, where were the hearing? If the whole were hearing, where were the smelling? . . . And if they were all one member, where were the body?" All Christian men are not called to the ministry. The carpenter and the blacksmith, the cotton manufacturer and the merchant, the physician and the lawyer, the artist, the scholar, and the statesman, are all as necessary as ourselves to the complete fulfilment of God's idea concerning the kingdom of heaven on earth. And all ministers do not receive the same spiritual gifts; for the work which they have to do is of different kinds. St. John as a saint and an apostle was not inferior either to St. Peter or to St. Paul ; but I do not know that we have any reason to suppose that his power as an evangelist was equal to theirs. It has been justly said that if St. Peter was the apostle of the circumcision, and St. Paul of the uncircumcision, St. John was the apostle of the Church. It may be that many of us are appointed to forms of service for which extraordinary evangelistic energy is not necessary. The spirit which leads some Christian men to speak disparagingly of all ministers who are not conspicuous for their evangelistic success, is a schismatic spirit. Our gifts vary with our functions, "that there should be no schism in the body; but that the members should have the same care one of another." Schism is schism still, even when it assumes the form of exceptional zeal for the evangelisation of the world.

The man on whom extraordinary evangelistic power is conferred must, as a rule, separate himself from the ordinary duties of the pastorate. He is appointed to other work, and must not decline it. His position is one of exceptional honour, and also of exceptional peril. He should be strengthened and sustained by the constant intercessions of the Church.

But even those of us who have reason to believe that God has called us to walk in obscurer paths, and to render Him a less brilliant service, may with reverence and humility ask for a larger measure of this special form of grace than most of us have received. God will not rebuke us for presumption if, in the presence of vast masses of human ignorance and misery and vice and irreligion, on which we are able to make hardly any impression, we entreat Him to grant us some of the force which He has granted in such a wonderful measure to illustrious evangelists. Or if for any reason this cannot be, we may still implore Him to bestow it on some of our brethren. Whether the work is done by ourselves or by others, it matters not; but we ought to pray incessantly that the work may be done.

Meanwhile, our duty is plain. It is for us to work with the strength we have, and to work devoutly and energetically. Dissatisfaction with our present service, a want of fidelity in the use of the gifts we have already received, will incapacitate us for service which may seem to us more urgently demanded, and will lessen the spiritual power which we actually possess. "To him that hath shall be given, and he shall have more abundance; but whosoever hath not, from him shall be taken away even that he hath."

LECTURE VIII.

PASTORAL PREACHING.

GENTLEMEN,—In the course of a very few years most of you will be pastors of Churches. I trust that you will enter upon your ministry with a right conception of the relations between yourselves and your people. Some ministers appear to think that Churches are founded in order to provide salaries for men who wish to master recent speculations on the Origin of Species and the Descent of Man, or to study at their leisure Auguste Comte and Herbert Spencer, or to make themselves familiar with German literature, and to form a judgment on the movement of German philosophical thought from Kant to Schopenhauer. There are other men who seem to believe that Churches exist to enable them to cultivate and to display their own remarkable genius, and that church buildings are erected to assist them to win a reputation. In the discourses which they are good enough to deliver every week, they suppose that they will discharge their duty if they report the results of their private studies, and show with what richness of imagination, what humour, what wit, what originality of thought, what beauty and vigour of style they can discuss any moral or religious subject in which they happen to feel a personal interest. These men are often betrayed by their immeasurable egotism and intellectual conceit into the most grotesque follies. Their sense of the immense importance of everything that concerns themselves and their sermons appears in their bearing and in their conversation in private, and not unfrequently finds its expression in the pulpit. Unhappily a preacher of this kind, if he has any power—no matter how inconsiderable—too often attracts a number of foolish people, who confirm him in the opinion that he is one of the greatest and most distinguished of mankind, and that his sermons take rank with the great historical events of the century. I shall not be so discourteous as to suppose that it is necessary to warn you against the grosser kinds of ministerial selfishness; but I trust that you will always remember that ministers exist for Churches—not Churches for ministers.

There is a certain measure of respect due from the people to their pastor; you are most likely to receive it if you do not claim it; you will never receive it at all if you forget that there is a certain measure of respect due from the pastor to the people. There is an authority belonging to the man who holds the ministerial office—an authority hard to define, but the recognition of which is essential to the peace of the Church and to its vigorous action. This authority will be most frankly and loyally conceded if you do not ostentatiously assert it. It will be refused if you do not habitually recognise the authority belonging to the Church.

One of your first objects should be to secure the confidence of your people. They will get very little good from your preaching unless they trust you. You and they are to work together; mutual trust is indispensable if you are to work together happily. To secure their confidence it is not enough that you deserve it. There are some young ministers who are upright, unselfish, chivalrous, devout, loyal to Christ, and who yet put a very severe strain on the generosity of their congregations. They thoughtlessly and wantonly provoke suspicion. So far as the substance of their creed is concerned, it is precisely identical with the creed of the people to whom they are preaching. But the form is different; and by their incessant attacks on what they suppose to be the unsatisfactory form in which the truth is commonly held, they create the impression that they reject the truth itself. This is sheer folly. The truth is greater than their particular intellectual conception and definition and theory of it. This they seem to forget, and the result is that they surround themselves with an atmosphere of distrust. They ought to make it clear that they have no new gospel to preach, though they may preach it in a new language. And even if, in connection with the central and fundamental truths of the Christian faith, many of their people hold what they believe to be pernicious errors, they will act wisely if, before attacking the errors, they have placed their own loyalty to the truth beyond suspicion.

Most of you, as I have said, are to be pastors of Churches—not missionaries or evangelists. You will have to preach to congregations largely composed of persons who already confess the authority of the Lord Jesus Christ, and who are trying to live a Christian life. The work of the evangelist and the work of the pastor are not, indeed, so different in fact as they are in theory; for many sermons which have for their direct aim the conversion of men who have not yet come home to God, strengthen the faith and increase the religious earnestness of those who have lived for thirty or forty years in the light of God's presence; and, on the other hand, sermons which are intended to give courage and guidance to those who are already seeking "by patient continuance in well-doing . . . for glory, honour, and immortality," sometimes alarm the conscience, and touch the heart of the impenitent. But it is quite clear that you would make a grave mistake if you always preached as though no one in your congregation had ever heard of the gospel before. As pastors, you will have to instruct your Churches in religious truth and duty.

In England there is an impression that modern sermons are generally defective in the element of instruction. Whether the impression is correct or not, I cannot tell; if it is, I think that the fault lies with the Churches themselves as well as with the preachers. If there is to be teaching in the pulpit, there must be intellectual activity in the pew; and there are some good Christian people in England who have yet to learn that they ought to serve God not only "with the spirit," but "with the understanding also." One Sunday morning, when I was a lad, I heard an excellent minister offer the prayer that God would grant the congregation during that day "intellectual repose," and I am inclined to think that very many of the people silently said Amen. It may be different in America, but with us there are many congregations that seem to have lost the habit of caring for solid teaching. Describe a thunderstorm, or a cataract, or a shipwreck; move them to tears by a touching story of human sorrow; give wings to your fancy, and carry the people far away into quiet glens, where the bright waters murmur softly over their rocky bed, where the foxglove blossoms, where the bee hums among the wild thyme, and the gorgeous dragon-fly hovers over the fern, and they think you one of "the finest preachers" in the country, though they are no wiser when the sermon ends than when it began. God forbid that I should depreciate the music of graceful speech, or the beauty and pomp of an imaginative eloquence; but for a nation's life, corn-fields and rich pastures are more precious than the romantic beauty of lonely lakes or the stern sublimity of the mountains which rise above them; and that preaching is barren and worthless which has no other object than to excite transient emotion, to stimulate the imagination, or to gratify the fancy.

It is not our business to get a reputation for being "fine preachers;" and if we are honest enough, manly enough, and, above all, Christian enough, to care less about winning a hasty and transient popularity than about doing real service to the Church, I believe that there is no congregation whose taste is so hopelessly corrupt, and whose intellectual life is so completely demoralised, that it may not be trained to value sermons which are full of instruction. All that is necessary is that the preacher should have courage, earnestness, patience, and a moderate amount of skill. He must not attempt too much at first; he must not preach dry sermons; he must learn how to teach—an art which can be acquired only by practice; and then he will find that to create in his congregation a keen interest in ethical and religious truth is less difficult than, perhaps, he supposed. I do not mean that sermons addressed to Christian people should be simply didactic. The formation of right moral habits and the discipline of the spiritual life should be the supreme objects of pastoral preaching; but ethical and religious knowledge is worth having for its own sake, and in the absence of it we have no reason to look for the development of the higher forms of moral and spiritual character.

In the Holy Scriptures we have the record of a long succession of supernatural revelations. Have we any reason to believe that even intelligent Christian men and women read the Scriptures intelligently? Do not many excellent persons seem to suppose that if they read a chapter in the Bible, whether they understand it or not, they have performed a religious duty, and are certain to receive religious benefit? In the Epistles, and even in the Gospels—to say nothing of the Old Testament prophecies — are there not many words, many phrases, whole sentences, long paragraphs, to which people who have been reading the Bible all their lives attach no meaning at all? When they are reading chapters with which they are most familiar, do they not come to crevasse after crevasse, over which they have to leap as best they can? And yet these very people have been listening twice a week for thirty or forty or fifty years to the discourses of men whose function it is to explain, illustrate, and enforce the contents of Holy Scripture.

Something might be done to lessen this ignorance if the lessons which commonly have a place in the order of public worship were selected more systematically, and were read with greater care. I acknowledge that to read the Bible well is not easy. The way in which our Bibles are printed creates a mechanical difficulty of a kind more serious than might be imagined: it would be hard to read Macaulay or Addison well if the "History of England" and the "Spectator" were cut up into verses. There is a graver difficulty. Our authorised version has great merits; but even when the translation is accurate and intelligible, the English is not the English of our own times. The structure of the sentences and the order of the words differ from the modern structure and the modern order. The style which we can read most easily and naturally is the style in which we and the people about us are constantly writing and speaking. This is not the style of the English Bible, and hence we find it hard to read the Bible with the right emphasis and the true cadence.

I have heard several men who read the Bible well; I never heard but one who read it supremely well. This was the late Mr. Dawson, of Birmingham, to whom I referred in a former lecture. To quote words of my own from a recent article in the *Nineteenth Century*:[1]—" It was genuine reading, not dramatic recitation — the dramatic recitation of the Bible is irreverent and offensive. But if he was reading a narrative he read it, not indeed as if he were telling the story himself, but as if he, too, had seen what he was reading about, and as if, while he read, the whole story lived again in his imagination and in his heart. If he was reading a psalm, he read it, not as some men read a psalm—as though they had written it—which is the dramatic style, and which seems to me false in art and morally presumptuous; but while he was reading you felt as if the words of the Psalmist recalled to him the brightest and the saddest passages in his own history, and as if these personal experiences naturally led him to read with a tone and an emphasis which were in perfect sympathy with the Psalmist's thought and feeling." To read in this way is not possible to most of us. It requires a rare combination

[1] *Nineteenth Century*, August, 1877.

of powers. But we should try to do our best. If we master the meaning of the passages we intend to read in public; if we so fully enter into the spirit of what we are reading that the printed book vanishes, and the story it tells comes to us fresh from the man that wrote it; if we read a psalm as though we ourselves had heard it from the lips of David, and as if the broken tones in which he confessed his sin, or the triumphant joy with which he spoke of the goodness of God, were still lingering in our ears; if we read a prophecy of Isaiah's with the feeling which the words would excite if we ourselves had listened to him while he was denouncing the crimes of his contemporaries and predicting the glories of the future kingdom of God; and if we read a passage from St. Paul's Epistle to the Galatians with that perfect sympathy with the sorrow and anger of the Apostle which will be created by a vivid realisation of his fierce conflict with the Judaizers; if, in short, by a vigorous imaginative effort we place ourselves by the very side of the men who wrote the Bible, see what they saw and feel what they felt, our mere reading of the Scriptures will throw an intense light on every passage that the people understood before, and will often bring out the meaning of passages which they had been accustomed to pass over as being quite unintelligible.

When I began my ministry it was my custom to preach expository sermons, in which I carefully explained and illustrated, clause by clause, verse by verse, a group of chapters or a complete book of Holy Scripture. Of late I have adopted what seems to me a better method. In the earlier part of the service I read a dozen or twenty verses—sometimes more, sometimes less—of the book I am expounding, beginning, of course, where I left off on the previous Sunday, and often prefacing the reading with a brief summary of what has gone before. Sometimes I venture to make a change in the translation, if I am quite sure that the translation is inaccurate, or that the change will make the meaning plainer or more vivid. If there are any sentences which are at all obscure, I give brief explanatory comments. If there are any allusions which ordinary people are not likely to notice, and which it is necessary to recognise in order to catch the writer's thought, I illustrate these allusions. When the whole passage is clear and intelligible, I read it without explanatory comments, for to explain what requires no explanation will perplex people instead of instructing them. Even in this case I often fasten on a particular verse or a particular phrase, and show how it annihilates some common error, or strengthens the evidence of some great truth, or rebukes some sin, or suggests a solemn or pathetic motive to the exercise of some Christian virtue.

The text of the sermon is selected from the passage which I have read, unless the passage would receive effective illustration from a text taken from another part of the Bible. If the passage is a consecutive argument in support of any doctrine, or an exhortation to the discharge of a moral or religious duty, or the expression of any sentiment or emotion—this doctrine, duty, emotion, or sentiment, is generally the subject of the sermon. If the passage treats of a succession of truths or duties, it is sometimes my endeavour to show how they are related to each other; sometimes I take one of them and leave the rest. Occasionally the sermon consists of a review of the contents of three or four chapters which have been read on previous Sundays. Sometimes when I have finished a book I have given a summary of the whole of it. I found that a summary of the Epistle to the Galatians was quite as exciting as a fiery pamphlet on some question of modern party politics.

The advantages of this method of exposition over that which I used to follow in the earlier years of my ministry seem to me to be very great. It is possible to get over the ground more rapidly. I never made such slow progress as the German exegetical professor, who, after lecturing on the Book of Isaiah for rather more than twenty years, had reached the middle of the second chapter; but I have the impression that I was two or three years getting through the first eight chapters of the Epistle to the Romans. With my present method I began the Epistle in April, 1876, reached the end of the eighth chapter in October of the same year, though I had been away for six weeks in the summer, and in February, 1877, the Epistle was finished.

This method of exposition seems to me more effective, as well as more rapid. Our practice of preaching from texts has accustomed people to try what they can discover in single sentences, and even single phrases, of the Bible, and to disregard the general current and structure of the argument or history: the minute exposition of clause after clause will confirm their evil habit. They seem to think that the best way to get a right conception of the Rhine, or of the Falls of Niagara, is to examine separate drops of the water under a microscope. The expository method which I have followed for some years past is likely, I think, to lead people to read the Bible as they read other books, and to look not merely at separate thoughts and fragments of separate thoughts, at isolated facts and the most insignificant circumstances connected with isolated facts, but at facts and thoughts in masses, and as they are grouped by the Scriptural writers themselves.

Exposition will do something to protect you from the desultoriness and want of method which is one of the gravest faults of our modern preaching, and which is one of the chief causes that it conveys so little definite and systematic instruction; but the fault is so serious that you ought, I think, to guard against it in other ways. Once, at least, in the course of a year, a Christian preacher should preach a sermon on such topics as the Humanity of our Lord, His Divinity, the Atonement, Justification by Faith, the Personality and

Work of the Holy Spirit, Regeneration, Prayer, the Future Judgment, and its awful and glorious results. We assume that persons who are accustomed to read the Bible and to listen to Christian preaching are sure to have a just conception of these great elementary truths. But the incidental allusions to them which occur in our sermons, the fragmentary illustrations of them which are suggested by texts in which they are presented under a special aspect, the references we make to them in order to enforce moral and spiritual duties, will never enable the people to form a clear and definite conception of them. It is a good habit to draw up at the beginning of the year a list of topics of this kind, on which we ought to preach before the year runs out, to refer to it from time to time, and when we preach upon any of the selected subjects, to write the date against it.

Both in your expository and in your doctrinal preaching it will be necessary to remember that the interest which you feel in certain intricate and difficult questions is largely the result of your professional studies. Some young preachers forget this. They have been investigating the controversies which culminated in the Council of Nicæa; or they have tried to master the philosophy of the theologians of Alexandria; or they have been reading Thomas Aquinas; or working hard at Turretin, Mæstricht, and Episcopius; or they have become penetrated with the spirit and method of Schleiermacher; or, at least, they have been studying closely the writings of American and English authors whose speculations are as yet unfamiliar to most educated men who are not professional theologians. As the result of their reading, and of their strenuous thinking on the deeper questions of theological science, they have a vehement interest in controversies which to large numbers of their hearers appear trivial or are absolutely unintelligible. To introduce controversies of this kind into the pulpit is preposterous. No genius or eloquence will induce most of your people to care for them.

I know what your reply will be. You will say that these controversies ultimately affect our way of conceiving the most elementary truths of the Christian faith. It is equally true that certain difficult branches of astronomical science have a great deal to do with the navigation of a ship, and that the latest biological speculations may throw a great deal of light on the growth of barley and the breeding of sheep. But it does not follow that a man must be a great astronomer before he can be qualified to take the command of a White Star or a Cunard steamer; nor does it follow that a man must master the latest books on biology before he can be a good farmer. The scientific theology which as a minister you have to master for yourself is something different from the popular and practical theology which alone you can teach your people — no matter how intelligent, no matter how cultivated they may be. You must be willing to accumulate a large amount of learning of which you can make no display in the pulpit, and to carry on long and laborious processes of thought which will make no show in your sermons.

What is true of doctrine is also true of exegesis. In Meyer's "Commentary on the Epistle to the Romans" he is incessantly discussing and refuting the interpretations of Hofmann ; but the people in your congregation never heard of Hofmann, and Hofmann's interpretations are never likely to occur to them. For you to discuss Hofmann's exegesis in the pulpit, because it has interested you in your study, would be to show that you had yet to learn the most elementary principles of the art of teaching.

But as a pastor you will be very much more than a teacher. You will have to cultivate the religious life of your people. This will be one of your gravest duties, and it will be one that ought to occasion you the most anxious thought. It must have occurred to you already that in the history of the Church the spiritual life has at different times and in different countries taken very different forms. The deep, central elements of sorrow for sin, consciousness of spiritual weakness apart from the life and strength of God, trust in the Divine mercy, love for Christ, earnest desire to do the Divine will, have been present everywhere and always. But just as a flower varies in the form of its leaf and the tint of its blossom according to the soil in which it is planted and the climate with which it is surrounded, so these permanent elements of the

Christian life have manifested themselves in different types of character according to the influences which have controlled and stimulated their development. Unless you believe—which would surely be somewhat presumptuous — that in the Church to which you happen to belong the religious life has at last assumed its perfect form, you will be anxious to learn in what it differs from the deepest and most vigorous piety of other Churches, other countries, and other centuries. Your sermons, your prayers, your intercourse with your people, will largely determine the colour and complexion of their religious character. The truths upon which you preach most frequently, the advice which you give to your congregation about the culture of devout affections and the formation of moral and spiritual habits, the characteristic elements and prevailing spirit of your public prayers, must powerfully affect for good or evil the growth of their religious life. You may give it too much sunshine or too much shade; you may shelter it too much, or may expose it to winds too rough and cold; you may let it grow too luxuriantly, or may prune it with too relentless a hand.

Would it not be wise to study the principal types of the spiritual life as they are represented in the few great devotional books which have won their way to the very hearts of Christian men? I refer to such books as Augustine's "Confessions," the "De Imitatione," Francis de Sales' "Devout Life," the "Spiritual Exercises" of Ignatius, Jeremy Taylor's "Holy

Living," Pascal's "Pensées," Richard Baxter's "Saint's Rest," John Bunyan's "Grace Abounding" and "Pilgrim's Progress." You might extend your reading to such books as Bishop Hall's "Christ Mystical," John Owen's "Spiritual-Mindedness," John Howe's "Blessedness of the Righteous," Law's "Spiritual Call," and Doddridge's "Rise and Progress." If there are any books of the same popular kind which have exerted a similar influence on the religious life of the Churches of this country, these too should receive your careful attention. Their popularity is a proof that they represent the religious ideal which fascinated the popular mind, and that their writers were in the main stream of the popular life and sympathies.

Among the considerations which books like these would suggest, will be the different results produced by the different degrees of prominence which have been given at different times to particular elements of the Christian creed. The great truths concerning the nature of God—such as the Trinity and the doctrines implicated in the Incarnation; the great truths concerning human redemption—such as the Atonement and Justification; the great truths concerning the personal realisation of redemption—such as the New Birth through the power of the Holy Ghost; have all at various times and in various places exerted supreme influence over the development of the religious life; and it is an inquiry full of interest to discover the varying results.

There are inquiries of another kind which will be

suggested by such books as those to which I have referred. You will be led to investigate the true limits within which self-examination should be confined, and the evils which the soul suffers from habitual introversion. You will consider how far asceticism is a legitimate and healthy aid to Christian living—that is, how far we may attempt to escape from sin by avoiding the occasions of sin, and how far we should trust for safety to the victorious power of the higher life of the soul, or, rather, to the victorious power of the Spirit of Christ. You will ask what are the natural and inevitable effects of certain spiritual maxims which have been accepted as self-evident by many eminent saints—as that the love of God is the only right motive of human action, a maxim which appears to me to be a direct impeachment of the righteousness of Him who gave us this strangely complicated nature, and a formal repeal of the law that in addition to loving God we are to love our neighbour as ourselves. You will consider to what extent conflicting theological systems such as Calvinism and Arminianism have received a practical verification from their effects on the spiritual life; what are the truths which, concealed under monstrous errors like that of Transubstantiation, have exerted a wonderful and ennobling influence on many devout souls; what are the causes which have given to Methodism its fervour, to Quakerism its practical Christian benevolence, and to the best type of Anglicanism its sobriety and reverence.

These studies will give depth and energy to your own religious earnestness. They will save you, in the temper and spirit of your religious life, from that which in the intellectual life has been called Provincialism. They will protect you from being mastered and fascinated by writers and preachers who from time to time produce a very powerful impression by the exhibition of isolated aspects of spiritual truth which, because they are isolated, have many of the effects of the worst and most pernicious errors.

These studies will have a most important relation to your preaching. They will enrich your knowledge of the laws, the perils, and the triumphs of the spiritual life, and they will do something to prevent you from treating the spiritual life of your people unwisely. There are, I believe, few congregations, at least in England, in which some persons may not be found whose religious nature has received serious and permanent injury from the very intensity of earnestness with which they have endeavoured to translate into practice false ideals of Christian character, empirical theories of the nature of holiness, and artificial methods of spiritual discipline. These unhappy people are likely to enter into the kingdom of heaven halt and maimed through the want of larger spiritual wisdom on the part of their religious teachers. Our work lies with the soul of man in its Divine relations, and we shall not do our work intelligently and effectively unless we give a considerable measure of time and thought to the investigation of the various phases which the spiritual life has assumed in the history of Christendom.

It is hardly necessary for me to remind you that for the Divine ideal of Christian character our ultimate authority is the New Testament. We have no right to be satisfied with striving to create in ourselves or others those forms of moral and spiritual excellence which happen to be sustained by the tradition and the general sentiment of the Church of which we are members, or which have kindled our imagination as they are illustrated in the writings and lives of the saints of other Churches. You will study, both for your own sake and for the sake of your people, the life of the Lord Jesus Christ, which is at once the law and the promise of Christian perfection; and you will endeavour so to preach that your people shall "abide" in Him by faith, by love, and by loyal obedience to His commandments. You will also endeavour to reconstruct for yourselves that conception of the Christian character which is suggested by the precepts, the prayers, the thanksgivings, and the incidental disclosures of the personal life of the apostles, in the epistles of the New Testament.

We ought not to take it for granted that most Christian people know what they ought to be, and that all they need is constancy and strength to live up to their knowledge. Some important elements seem to be suppressed in the common ideal of Christian perfection. Take a single illustration. In St. Paul's account of "the fruits of the Spirit," he gives the first place to Love, and we acknowledge that a Christian man who has an unloving, ungenerous, unkindly heart, is hardly a Christian at all. But he gives the second place to Joy, and it is my impression that there are many of us who seldom think of Joy as a necessary and indispensable element in our conception of a saint. We ask God to forgive us for our evil thoughts and evil temper, but rarely, if ever, ask Him to forgive us for our sadness. Joy is regarded as a happy accident of the Christian life, an ornament and a luxury, rather than a duty. We forget that we are commanded to "rejoice evermore." It should be one of the objects of our ministry to deepen and heighten the joy of Christian hearts, as well as to strengthen reverence for God's authority and to increase the fervour of zeal for His glory.

In trying to cultivate Christian perfection, we must not satisfy ourselves with censuring people for being imperfect. You will not do much towards sanctifying your people by scolding them. Perpetual fault-finding does no good: it is bad for children, bad for servants, and it is bad for Churches. It is mere indolence, and it is sometimes ill-temper, which leads a minister, to indulge in perpetual condemnation. Nor will you do much if you merely tell the people over and over again that they ought to be better. Men are not to be worried into goodness. You remember Mrs. Poyser's description of the two parsons of Hayslope. "You know she would have her word about everything—she said Mr. Irwine was like a good meal

o' victual, you were the better for him without
thinking on it; and Mr. Ryde was like a dose o'
physic, he gripped you and worreted you, and after
all he left you much the same."[1] Mr. Ryde has
many followers—preachers who give their congregations all "physic" and no "victual." The physic
may be excellent of its kind, admirable if prescribed
occasionally. But physic, week after week, all the year
round; physic every Sunday morning at eleven, and
every Sunday evening at half-past six; physic again
at the prayer-meeting on Wednesday or Thursday
night—ugh!—it is intolerable. It is pernicious as
well as offensive. It is enough to ruin the health of
the most vigorous Church.

Let your congregation have the "Bread of Life."
Instead of merely complaining to them of the absence
of brotherly kindness, preach sermons which are likely
to make them more vividly conscious that they are
brethren in Christ. Instead of satisfying yourself with
finding fault with them for their want of zeal, ask how
you can stimulate it. Speak sharp words occasionally
in condemnation of covetousness, but return again
and again to those parts of the gospel which inspire
generosity. Deplore, if you must, the inconstancy
of many Christian people in right-doing, the languor
of their spiritual affections, their indifference to the
supreme objects of the Christian life; but remember
that mere lamentations will work no deliverance for
them. You must consider by what truths, by what

[1] George Eliot: "Adam Bede," p. 157. (One volume edition.)

method and spirit of teaching, you can develop among them all the energetic forces and all the noble excellences of the Christian character.

I wonder whether you have in America any Christian people who resent what are contemptuously described as "Moral" sermons. There were, I believe, many such people in England thirty years ago, and though it has never been my ill fortune to meet with them, I am told that a few of their descendants may still be found in some obscure Churches. Whether sermons of this kind are resented or not, they are necessary. The distinction between moral duties and religious duties is a convenient one, but it is misleading. The very same authority that requires us to believe in the Lord Jesus Christ requires us to be just, truthful, temperate, and industrious. The practice of the common virtues is as essential a part of Christian obedience as the habit of prayer and the culture of the spiritual affections. There may be morality where there is no religion; but that there should be religion where there is no morality, is impossible. The moral law is the law of God.

It is therefore just as much our duty to illustrate and enforce the obligations of morality as it is to insist on the necessity of believing the gospel. We have to teach men the will of God; and we have no more right to suppress that part of the will of God which relates to duties which are called moral than we have to suppress that part of the will of God which relates to duties which are called religious.

If we require any authoritative sanction for moral preaching we may appeal to the example of our Lord Jesus Christ. But the people who object to preaching of this kind would probably reply that what they delight to call the "Old Covenant," and the "Covenant of Works," was not abolished till Christ died for the sins of men, rose from the dead, and ascended into heaven. They have a secret conviction that though the Sermon on the Mount might be very well for Jews, it is not spiritual enough for Christians; and I think that if they had their wish, the first three Gospels, if not the fourth, would be bound up with the Old Testament instead of with the New. Well, we must meet men on their own ground, and if the authority of Christ is not decisive, we must ask them whether St. Paul misunderstood the spirit and genius of the Christian dispensation. If moral teaching is out of place in a modern sermon, had it any right to a place in an apostolic epistle? St. Paul wrote about lying, anger, malice, covetousness; about the duties of masters and servants, parents and children. It is difficult to understand why we should be guilty of a "legal" spirit when we preach against the vices which St. Paul condemned, or enforce the duties which St. Paul commanded.

It may be said that St. Paul was writing to people who had been recently converted from heathenism, and whose consciences had not yet been trained to the recognition of the sinfulness of vices which were sanctioned by the common opinion of their heathen fellow-countrymen; and, like converts from heathenism in our own times, they did not discover at once the obligation of even those ordinary virtues which in Christian countries are enforced by the moral judgment of the whole community. It is unnecessary to consider to what extent it is true that the public opinion of Thessalonica, Colosse, and Ephesus approved the vices which St. Paul condemns in his letters to the Churches in those great cities. It is clear that St. Paul did not believe that faith in Christ rendered moral instruction unnecessary. And if the moral ideal of the Christians of apostolic times was corrupted and degraded by the false moral judgments of that heathen society with which they were in perpetual contact, we have to ask whether even in countries like America and England the ethics of public opinion are identical with the ethics of Christ? whether it can be assumed as a matter of course that no American and no Englishman has anything to learn from the moral teaching of the New Testament? The slightest knowledge of mankind is sufficient to prove to us that even in countries like our own it is possible for the conscience to be most imperfectly developed. In the world and in the Church men mean well and act badly. In both there is a lamentable ignorance of moral duty.

Where moral duty is recognised it is not always discharged, even by Christian people. Through force of habit, perhaps unconsciously, they distinguish between duty and duty. One duty they dare not neglect, another they neglect constantly without any keen compunction. Sins of one class they suppose to be utterly inconsistent with loyalty to Christ; sins of another class they have come to regard as being mere infirmities—infirmities to be regretted, infirmities which mar, no doubt, the perfection of Christian character; infirmities for which they need God's forgiveness; but still mere infirmities, which may be tolerated without imperilling their eternal salvation. Some habits their consciences condemn only occasionally; weeks and months go by and these habits are unrebuked. Some of Christ's moral precepts they seem to regard as " counsels of perfection," intended for great saints, but having no relation to the lives of common Christian people. Or they even suppose that there were some of His precepts which He never expected would be kept, and which were meant—not to give form to our righteousness—but to deepen our consciousness of sin. It is certain—we may learn it from observation, we may learn it from our personal experience—that the Divine life which comes to a man when he is regenerated does not at once transform the whole character. He may be guilty of many moral offences which his conscience does not condemn; or the authority of his conscience may be feeble, and he may make no serious effort to escape from moral habits which he knows are sinful. In our ethical preaching we must deal both with moral ignorance and with the want of moral earnestness.

We must be careful to avoid the tendency to dwell

exclusively on those virtues which Christianity redeemed from dishonour or from neglect, or which, through their nearer kinship to the characteristic spirit of the Christian faith, have flourished with exceptional vigour in the Christian Church. Humility, meekness, gentleness; the charity that "suffereth long and is kind, . . . envieth not, . . . beareth all things, believeth all things, hopeth all things, endureth all things ;" are specifically Christian virtues, and if we ever preach on morals these virtues are almost certain to receive attention. Nor are we likely to fail in insisting on the obligations of temperance and purity; for the traditional sentiment of the Church is irreconcilably hostile to the opposite vices. But there are virtues which Paganism recognised, and these are equally necessary to the completeness of the Christian character. To these, neither the teaching nor what may be called the public opinion of the Church has given adequate prominence, and it is part of our duty to reassert their authority. You will remember the account which Mr. John Stuart Mill gives in his Autobiography of the moral training which he received from his father. It was the training of a pagan. His father's moral convictions, as he tells us in the passage to which I am referring, were " wholly dissevered from religion," and " were very much of the character of those of the Greek philosophers." " My father's moral inculcations," says Mr. Mill, " were at all times mainly those of the ' Socratici viri :' justice, temperance (to which he gave a very extended application), veracity, perseverance; readiness to encounter pain, and especially labour; regard for the public good; estimation of persons according to their merits, and of things according to their usefulness; a life of exertion, in contradiction to one of self-indulgent ease and sloth."[1]

Throughout these lectures I have suffered under the disadvantage of knowing very little about the life of American Churches. From the evils with which I am familiar at home you may be free. But in England there are many Christian men and women who seem to ignore the obligation to cultivate these heathen virtues. They have no conception that a life of indolent ease is an unchristian life; that the instability of character—as distinguished from mere physical weakness—which betrays itself in a perpetual change of pursuit, and an incapacity to sustain for long together the pressure of any kind of work, is a moral fault; that cowardice is not meekness; that neglect of public duty and absorption in the quiet pleasures of home, instead of being a proof of unworldliness of spirit, is a proof of selfishness; that a man may be very kindly and yet very unjust, generous with his money and ungenerous in his spirit. Some people, in short, who pass for very good Christians would be very poor pagans. If you have people of this kind in America, you will feel the necessity of preaching on what we call the masculine virtues, although I have seen them quite as nobly developed in the lives of women as in the lives of men.

[1] John Stuart Mill: "Autobiography," pp. 46, 47.

For your ethical sermons you may find appropriate texts in the innumerable moral precepts both of the Old Testament and the New. You will also find in the biographical and historical incidents of the Bible admirable subjects for sermons of this kind. Rebekah's treatment of Jacob may bring home to parents the sin of parental partiality. Jacob's treachery to Esau will enable you to show that devout men may be guilty of the basest conduct to men who profess no religious earnestness. Joseph telling his dreams is an illustration of youthful vanity and conceit. The story of the spies you can use to condemn cowardice as well as unbelief. The chaotic history of the Jewish people during the time of the Judges is a warning to nations of the perils which threaten them when they shrink from the vigorous and thorough suppression of moral evils which threaten the unity and stability of the national life. The history of David and of Solomon is full of ethical instruction on every page. The history of Jeremiah is a perpetual condemnation of the popular intolerance of men who assert unwelcome truths. St. Paul's kindly words in the last chapter of the Epistle to the Romans — " Salute Tryphena and Tryphosa, who labour in the Lord. Salute the beloved Persis, which laboured *much* in the Lord "—may teach Christian people to repress their miserable jealousy when the work of others receives higher and warmer commendation than their own. And where can you find a more effective rebuke of that intense selfishness which takes the form of a morbid craving for sympathy, than in Epaphroditus, who, as St. Paul tells the Philippians, was "full of heaviness" because his friends at Philippi "had heard that he had been sick"? He had been in greater danger than they imagined, for "he was sick nigh unto death;" and yet it distressed him that his brethren should have known anything about his illness.

But we have not merely to deal with the details of moral conduct, with particular virtues and particular vices; we have to make clear to our congregations the ultimate laws and aims of the Christian life. There are many Christian people whose conception of the relation of Christ's authority to their common occupations and pursuits is fundamentally false. They call Christ their Master, and yet they seem to imagine that for six days in the week their time is their own, and that they are at liberty to work for themselves. The farmer, the builder, the manufacturer, suppose that after they have surrendered themselves to Christ as His "servants," His "slaves," they are just as free as they were before to carry on their business for their own profit, so long as they do not violate the laws of common morality. A sharp line is drawn between the Christian ministry and all other occupations. We ministers have a right to receive adequate support, but if it were our object to "make money" by the ministry, the universal sentiment of the Church would condemn us as profane and irreligious persons. It would be of no avail to plead that all the means we used were perfectly legitimate, that we violated no moral law, that we preached sound doctrine, tried hard to make bad men good and good men better: we should be told that we cannot serve Christ and Mammon, that if a minister sets his heart upon "making money" by his ministry he ceases to be a true servant of Christ.

Are *we* the servants of Christ, and are the people, at least for six days in the week, the servants of Mammon? Do we belong to Christ, and do they belong to themselves? Are we temples of the Holy Ghost — our whole life being set apart to sacred purposes, filled with the presence and glory of God—and are we to teach the people that their life—the greater part of it at least—is a mere store, or counting-house, or cotton-mill, and that they must be satisfied with having a little chapel built on at the end of it, covering only a seventh part of the site? I decline to be a party to that atrocious conspiracy against the prerogatives of the commonalty of the Church, which has invested the life of the priesthood with a sacredness that does not belong to the life of the people. We are all Christ's servants, though we have to serve Him in different ways. "By one Spirit are we all baptised into one body, whether we be Jews or Gentiles, bond or free," lawyers or physicians, artists or schoolmasters, manufacturers or farmers, merchants or ministers; "and have been all made to drink of one Spirit. For the body is not one member, but many."

It is our function, as ministers, to satisfy the wants and to contribute to the strength and joy of the higher life of man. But men have a physical as well as a spiritual nature. There are other wants than those which we are appointed to satisfy, and there are other forms of strength and joy than those to which we are appointed to contribute. The race would perish with hunger if all men gave themselves to "prayer and the ministry of the Word," and if there were none to "serve tables." We say that God opens His hand and satisfies the wants of every living thing. Behind the mystery of the life which is hidden in the seed, behind the fruitful qualities of the soil, behind the soft spring rains and the heat of the summer sun, we recognise the Divine presence and power. But if the harvest is God's gift, the farmer is God's servant. While he ploughs the ground and sows the seed and reaps the brown corn, he may give God thanks that he is engaged in no mere secular work. He and God are working together, and answering the prayers of men for "daily bread;" he is the minister of God's goodness, "attending continually upon this very thing." He serves God in the field, as we serve God in the study and in the pulpit. As it is our first duty to bring out of God's supernatural revelation whatever it can be made to yield for the spiritual life of man, it is his first duty to bring out of God's material world whatever it can be made to yield for the physical life of man. The farmer has to get his own living while he is providing for the wants of others; but this is true of the preacher; the ox is not to be muzzled that treadeth out the corn. But the preacher, if his heart is right, and if he understands the true idea of the ministry, does not work to "make money," but because God has appointed him to minister to the spiritual wants of mankind; and the farmer, if his heart is right, and if he understands the true idea of farming, does not work to "make money," but because God has appointed him to minister to the physical wants of mankind.

Every profession and occupation that men call secular becomes a good work and a part of the religious life when it is carried on in this spirit and with these aims. One man—perhaps he may be a Christian man—who has been a builder for thirty or forty years, and who has been, as the world says, "successful," has nothing to show except the hundred or two hundred thousand dollars which he has made out of his business. It was for this that he worked, and this is the net gain of his work. Another man in the same trade but with higher conceptions of it may have accumulated less or more, but his dollars are to him the least important result of his thirty or forty years in the building trade. He has been serving God all the time, and his true reward will come when he stands at last in God's presence to hear God's judgment on his service. Even now it is not his dollars which give him the greatest satisfaction. As he passes the schools and the churches which he built, it is pleasant to him to remember that he, too, has had a share in providing for the education of children and for the worship of God. As he lies awake on a winter's night, and hears the wind and the rain on the windows, he thinks of hundreds of houses built by himself, with strong walls and sound roofs, that are giving a shelter from the storm to sick people, and to aged men and women, and to boys and girls whose sound sleep the wind and the rain do not disturb, and he thanks God that he was permitted to do so good a work for mankind. What are the dollars, compared with the consciousness of having used life for a kindly purpose?

The artist who has worked at his art in the same temper has similar rewards. He may have received great prices for his pictures, and have become famous, but neither his wealth nor his fame is the chief source of his joy. He remembers the sunset which he saw on the sea twenty years ago—the magnificent masses of purple and the throbbing lines of fire in the heavens above, and the splendour that rested on the rocks and the water beneath. It was God who gave men that vision of glory, but had it not been for him it would have faded away from human memory for ever: the glory is still glowing on his canvas in the gallery of some remote city, and is filling men with wonder and delight. Every year he has spent many months among the corn-fields that lie round quiet New England villages, or on the banks of pleasant streams, or among the lonely hills, and he has taught men to see a loveliness and a majesty in God's works which they would never have seen for themselves. His paintings hang on the walls of city merchants, and are a perpetual refreshment to them. Engravings of them find their way into poor men's houses, and add something of grace and dignity to lives which are spent in exhausting toil. He has not lived in vain. God gave him noble work to do, and he has done it.

There is no legitimate trade which may not receive consecration. How charming a life, for instance, may be the life of the jeweller. He is employed by God to get precious stones from distant lands—diamonds and emeralds and sapphires—stones which God made for ornament and beauty. He sets them in gold curiously worked, and then they are ready to give a new brilliance to womanly loveliness which seemed already perfect, and to be the graceful expression and enduring memorial of human affection. The husband brings home the costly bracelet, and as the wife clasps it on her arm she is happy that after twenty years of marriage her husband's heart clings to her still. The child puts on her necklet, and thinks less of the pearls than of the dear love of the father who has given them to her. The young man, far from home, is strengthened in right doing by the face of his mother in his locket, or perhaps by a face which his mother, with a sigh, must be content should be dearer to him than her own. A jeweller's work is beautiful in itself; in its uses it is more beautiful still. He may thank God for appointing him to so pleasant a service.

Every trade and profession is vulgarised and debased, becomes " of the earth, earthy," when a man follows it selfishly and simply to make money; when a man accepts it as the service to which God has appointed him, for the advantage and happiness of the human race, it is exalted and transfigured, and takes its place among the activities of the kingdom of heaven.

In your Pastoral Preaching you ought not to omit to illustrate the law of Christ in relation to public duty. Perhaps you have sometimes met good people who informed you in a tone of spiritual self-complacency that they have never been in a polling-booth. They do not seem to understand that the franchise is a trust, and that it imposes duties. A secretary of state might as well make it a religious boast that he habitually neglected some of the work belonging to his department. The duties of an individual voter may be less grave than the duties of an official politician, but neglect in either case is a crime against the nation. I think it possible that the time may come when men who refuse to vote will be subjected to Church discipline, like men who refuse to pay their debts. The plea that the discharge of political duty is inconsistent with the maintenance of spirituality ought to be denounced as a flagrant piece of hypocrisy. It is nothing else. The men who urge it are not too spiritual to make a *coup* in cotton or coffee. Although they profess to be alarmed at the spiritual perils of the ballot-box and of an occasional hour in a political committee-room, they are not afraid that their spirituality will suffer if they spend eight hours every day in their store or their counting-house.

Their spirituality is of such a curious temper that it receives no harm from pursuits—no matter how secular—by which they can make money for themselves; but they are afraid of most disastrous consequences if they attempt to render any service to their country.

The selfishness of these men is as contemptible as their hypocrisy. They consent to accept all the advantages which come from the political institutions of the nation and from the political zeal and fidelity of their fellow-citizens. They are quite willing to hold United States bonds; they draw their dividends without any conscientious scruples; they send part of the money perhaps to the Board of Foreign Missions; the Sunday after they receive it they put an extra dollar into the plate at the Lord's Supper. But United States bonds would be as worthless as Turkish 6 per cents of '62 if thousands and tens of thousands of American citizens did not devote themselves with courage and earnestness to the maintenance of sound political principles and to the defence of your political institutions. People who are so very spiritual that they feel compelled to abstain from political life ought also to renounce the benefits which the political exertions of their less spiritual fellow-citizens secure for them. They ought to decline the services of the police when they are assaulted; they ought to refuse to appeal to such an unspiritual authority as a law court when their debts are not paid; and when a legacy is left them they ought piously to abstain from accepting it, for it is only by the intervention of public law that they can inherit what their dead friends have left them. For men to claim the right to neglect their duties to the State on the ground of their piety, while they insist on the State protecting their persons, protecting their property, and protecting from disturbance even their religious meetings in which this exquisitely delicate and valetudinarian spirituality is developed, is gross unrighteousness. It is as morally disgraceful as for a clerk to claim his salary from his employer after leaving other men to do the work for which his employer pays him. It is a repetition in another form of the crime which our Lord condemned in the Pharisees who declined to give assistance to their poor parents, and excused themselves by saying that what their parents might have expected from them they had devoted to God.

The public duties which you have to exhort your congregations to discharge are not exhausted when they have used their ballot-paper. In a free country every citizen should do something towards strengthening public opinion on behalf of what he believes to be wise and just political principles, and towards maintaining whatever political organisation will, in his judgment, place the administration of public affairs in the hands of upright and able men.

Nor is it only in the political life of this great Republic as a whole, or in the political life of their own State, that Christian men ought to be taught to take their fair share. Honest and effective municipal government lies at the very base of public freedom and public order. It is by the discharge of municipal duties that men are disciplined to the true political temper, to the sagacity, moderation, patience, and courage which are necessary for the right conduct of political affairs ; and it is by encouraging men to watch their local administration with keen interest, that public spirit is formed and strengthened.

The burdens which lie on those who take an active part in the government of a great city are very heavy. But the burdens must be accepted, and accepted by good men, or your common schools will be badly conducted, and the children will be badly taught ; your streets will be neither well drained nor well swept; and the health of the people will suffer ; your police will be inefficiently organised, and will fail to repress crime ; your public servants will be appointed by corrupt influence ; your finances will be plundered. For men who are able to serve the community by entering municipal corporations, to refuse to do it when their services are needed, is a dereliction of Christian duty. If they decline on the ground that the rough incidents of a popular election and the rough conflicts of public life are inconsistent with their spirituality, they should be taught that they are either suffering from an exceptional want of spiritual earnestness and vigour, and that they ought to become healthier and stronger ; or that their conception of the spiritual life is fundamentally false, and ought to be corrected ; or that they are playing the hypocrite, and that it is time for them to become honest men. If they decline through sheer indolence and want of interest in public affairs, they should be rebuked for their selfishness, and taught that the supreme law of the Christian life requires a man to "look not on his own things, but on the things of others."

When a Christian man accepts municipal or political office, it should be with the simple intention of serving the community. He has no right to think of his office as an instrument for increasing his own wealth, or for acquiring reputation, or for strengthening his personal influence. His office is a public trust, and should be used for the public good without any thought of private advantage.

It is our constant prayer that God's will may "be done on earth, even as it is done in heaven;" our preaching should be definitely directed to securing the fulfilment of this prayer. We fail if we merely induce men to accept a right creed. We fail if we do nothing more than create religious sentiment and stimulate religious emotion. We also fail if the authority of Christ is excluded from any province of human life. In England I fear that the Christian ministry itself is largely responsible for an unnatural and fatal reconciliation of practical atheism with Christian faith. In our preaching we have omitted to show the relation of Christian law to many of the most energetic forms of human activity. We have left what we have called the secular interests of mankind to be governed by secular aims and to be penetrated by a secular spirit, forgetting that if a man is a true servant of God he serves God always and everywhere, and that Christ came into the world to bring earth and heaven together. We have even neglected to insist on the Christian development of some of the most important elements of human character, and have led men to suppose that the more vigorous virtues—the very virtues which are most necessary in the actual business of life—derive no inspiration and force from the law and truth of Christ, and from the great hopes of the gospel. We have insisted on precise accuracy in the definition of difficult theological problems ; we have subjected spiritual experiences to a delicate analysis ; but we have been wanting either in the wisdom or the courage to insist that human life in all its length and breadth and height and depth belongs to Christ, and that no part of it can be withdrawn from His control without guilt. If we have asserted this in general terms, we have shrunk from illustrating in detail the relations of the law of Christ to the actual pursuits of men. We have supposed—some of us at least—that we have performed nearly all our duty in relation to the practical life of our people when we have discussed the legitimacy of balls and card-playing and the theatre, and other amusements of a similar kind, in which most of them could spend only insignificant fragments of their time. We have tithed " mint and anise and cummin, and have omitted the weightier matters of the law ; . . . these ought [we] to have done, and not to leave the others undone." From the cup of life we have strained out the gnat, and left our people to swallow the camel.

These fatal mistakes must be corrected, or the force of the Christian faith will be paralysed and its authority will cease to command reverence and awe. We have not to leave the world to itself, but to conquer it. God intends that Commerce, Science, Art, Literature, Politics, shall all be subjected to His law. Then, and not till then, will " the kingdoms of this world " become in deed and of a truth the kingdom of our Lord and of His Christ.

LECTURE IX.

THE CONDUCT OF PUBLIC WORSHIP: THE LIVING GOD: ORIGINALITY: THE PRESENCE OF CHRIST: CONCLUSION.

GENTLEMEN,—In this closing lecture I trust that you will allow me to speak on several topics, each of them of sufficient importance to claim an afternoon for itself. The time at my command has almost run out, but there are three or four subjects having no intimate and logical relation to each other on which I should like to say something before I bid you farewell.

First of all, I will speak of the Conduct of Public Worship. Before you have been very long in the ministry I think it very likely that your public prayers will occasion you great perplexity and humiliation. Your courage will, perhaps, fail altogether, and you will begin to ask whether your people would tolerate a liturgy. There is hardly a thoughtful minister of my own age, among my personal friends, who has not at times looked wistfully in that direction. Happily the traditions and instincts of our congregations have saved us from the mistake into which our weakness might have betrayed us. Reflection and experience have convinced me that it would be hardly possible to inflict a worse injury on the life and power of our Churches than to permit free, extemporaneous prayer to be excluded from our services or even to be relegated to an inferior position. We need not despair. We, too, have received the Holy Ghost. He did not forsake the Church when the great saints of former ages passed away; and if we rely on His inspiration, and devote to the substance, the spirit, and the form of this part of the service the thought and care which it ought to receive, our difficulties will soon be diminished, and perhaps in time they will disappear altogether.

The root of my own difficulties, and the root, as I think, of the difficulties of many of my friends, was a mistaken impression that extemporaneous prayer might include — in addition to its own excellences —the characteristic excellences of a liturgy. But we must make our choice. In extemporaneous prayer, the stateliness, the majesty, the æsthetic beauty of such a service as that of the Anglican Episcopal Church, and the power which it derives from venerable associations, are impossible. We must be content with simplicity, directness, pathos, reverence, fervour; and if we are less vividly conscious than those who use a liturgy that we are walking in the footsteps of the saints of other centuries, we may find compensation in a closer and more direct relation to the actual life of the men, women, and children who are waiting with ourselves for the mercy and help and pity of God. We lose less than we may gain.

But we shall gain nothing and lose everything if we do not remember the true purpose for which prayers are offered. They are not intended to afford a special form of gratification to men of taste who feel no awe in the presence of God's greatness, no distress at the remembrance of their sin, no strong desire for forgiveness and for strength to live a holy life, no deep sympathy with the sorrows and perils of mankind. They are intended to express to God the trouble and fear and trust of hearts which have learnt that their only hope for themselves and for all men is in Him, and to obtain from God those blessings which He has promised to bestow. Prayers are not works of art; they are great spiritual acts.

In the earlier years of your ministry most of you will, I think, find it wise to make definite preparation for your prayers as well as for your sermons. I am not sure that even those of us who have been in the ministry longest have any right to neglect that preparation.

A great part of the material for our prayers we may derive from God's thoughts about ourselves and the people with whom we have to pray. God's idea of our life, the idea which He wants us to fulfil, is the law of our conduct; and we may be certain that God wants to give us the light and strength we need to keep this law. If the moral and spiritual perfection for which we are longing is nothing more than a dream of our own, then our confidence in God's willingness to help us is not likely to be very firm. We may trust God when we ask Him for power to obey a law which we accept from Him; we have no right to be sure that He will enable us to obey a law which we have constructed for ourselves. The love of God as well as His law—if His law and His love can be separated—will also suggest materials for prayer. The love of God found its supreme expression in the incarnation and the death of our Lord Jesus Christ; but the promises of Christ, the large hopes of prophets, psalmists, and apostles, the consolation which God has given in times of trouble to those who have trusted in Him, the defence which He has given in times of danger, the victories which He has given over strong temptation, the light in hours of perplexity and darkness, also illustrate the wealth of the Divine goodness, and teach us what we may pray for. There is no height of joy, no depth of peace, no intimacy of communion with Himself, which God does not desire to make ours. When we ask for them we may not consciously receive them at once, but it does not follow that He has refused to answer us. A child who wants to go home is answered as soon as his father's consent is put on the wires; but if the child is several thousand miles away, it may be weeks and even months before he finds himself under his father's roof. And, perhaps, after the consent has been given he may shrink from the long journey over sea and land; his home-sickness may pass off; he may prefer to stay where he is; and so his father's arrangements for his return may come to nothing. It sometimes happens so with us. We ask God for great blessings, but when He answers us, and the path which leads to the blessings lies open before us, we have ceased to care for them, and we refuse to take a single step to reach them; or soon after we have started we grow weary and turn back; and then we wonder that our prayers are not answered.

We may derive materials for prayer from the lives of our congregations — materials of inexhaustible variety. There is always sin to be confessed, sorrow which God alone can soothe and comfort, weakness that needs Divine support; and there is always happiness for which we should offer thanksgiving. But we must be very indolent or else we must be cursed with a dull and unsympathetic nature, if we are satisfied with a vague and general remembrance of the sin, the sorrow, the weakness, the joy, which cloud or brighten the lives of our people. In our preparation for our public prayers we should think of the people one by one, and make all their trouble and all their gladness our own. There are the children—children whose faces are pale from recent sickness or accident, or whose health is never robust and whose spirits are never high; children that are strong and healthy, with pure blood in their veins, with sound limbs, and who are always as happy as birds in summer time; children that are wretched because they have no kindness at home; children that want to do well, but who have inherited from their parents a temperament which makes it hard for them to be gentle, obedient, industrious, courageous, and kindly; and children to whom with the earliest dawn of reason there came a purer light from the presence of God, and to whom it seems natural and easy to be good.

We should think of the young men and women, with their ardour, their ambition, their vanity; their dreams of the joy and glory which the hastening years are to bring them; their generous impulses; the inconstancy in right doing which troubles and perplexes them; the disappointments which have already embittered the hearts of some, and made them imagine that for them life has no gladness left; the consciouness of guilt which already rankles in the hearts of others; the frivolity, the selfishness, of which some are the early victims; the hard fight which some are carrying on with temptations which are conquered but not crushed; the doubts which are assaulting the faith of others; the bright heaven of happiness in which some are living, happiness which comes from the complete satisfaction of the strongest human affections; the still brighter heaven which is shining around others who are already living in the light of God.

The enumeration, if I attempted to go through with it, would occupy hours. We have to think of aged people who have outlived their generation, and whose strength is gradually decaying, in lonely and desolate houses, uncheered by the presence of living affection, and saddened by memories of the dead. We have to think of the men and women whose children are growing up about them, and on whom the cares of life are resting heavily. We have to think of places which are vacant in some seats because a boy is at college, or has gone to sea, or has just entered a house of business in a distant city, or because a girl has been sent away to recover health under some kindlier sky. There are other places vacant for other reasons: those who once filled them have forsaken and forgotten the God of their fathers. We have to think of families in the congregation whose fortunes have been ruined; and of orphans and widows; and of the young bride whose orange flowers have hardly faded; and of the young mother whose heart is filled, all church time, with happy thoughts about her first-born at home.

There are the impenitent of all ages; and there are those whose consciences have been recently struggling to assert the authority of God, and whose hearts have been recently touched by the love of Christ, but who have not yet fully committed themselves to Christ's service; and there are those who are thrilling with the unutterable joy of their first access to God; and there are some, perhaps, who are becoming weary of the great endeavour to keep God's commandments perfectly, and who are drifting back to a life of religious indifference.

There is the work of the Church to pray for. And we should not think of the work as though it were done by a great machine. We should remember the living men and women who are doing it—some of them glowing with the heat of early enthusiasm; some of them beginning to be disheartened because success does not come as soon as they hoped it would; some of them with the firm and settled habits of labour which have been formed by many years of loyal and faithful endeavour to serve Christ. There are neighbouring Churches to pray for; there are missions at home and abroad, among Pagans, among Mahometans, among the adherents of corrupt Churches. The intellectual life of the nation, and its social and political condition, will also suggest materials for prayer. You pray for your President, and for the political men at Washington, and for the governors and political authorities of your separate States; but you should also pray for your schoolmasters and schoolmistresses, and for your judges and magistrates. Sometimes, surely, you should remember the criminals in your gaols and the criminals at large, and the compassionate and noble labours of the good men and women that are trying to reform them. Gentlemen, I believe in free prayer. You will believe in it too, if your hearts are open to all the sorrow and gladness, weakness and strength, conflict and hope, glory and shame, of the lives of men, and if you have a large faith in the love of God.

In addition to preparing the substance of your prayers, it is legitimate, and some of you may find it necessary, to think of their form. You may collect passages from the Psalms, the Prophets, and the Epistles, which, in loftier words than you can command, express adoration of God's majesty and holiness and glory. You may arrange the order in which you will use "exceeding great and precious promises." You may occasionally prepare the language as well as the substance of special petitions, confessions, and thanksgivings. Above all, you will remember that unless your own spirit is disciplined for communion with God, all other preparation will be of no avail.

In England, after all that has been written on Congregational Singing, during the last twenty-five or thirty years, I doubt whether we even now appreciate the importance of Psalmody in relation to the spiritual life and temper of the Church; and in Psalmody I include both hymns and the music to which they are sung. Some one said, "Let me write the songs of a nation, and I do not care who makes the laws;" and I should be inclined to say, "Let me write the hymns and the music of the Church, and I care very little who writes the theology."

Heresy and Orthodoxy alike have in past ages discovered and used the power of sacred song. Arius, though a keen and acute controversialist, did not rely on his logic alone for the spread of his doctrine on the person of Christ, but wrote songs for sailors, millers, and pilgrims. Chrysostom, when bishop of Constantinople, saw the crowds of people that were gathered at night and early dawn, in porticoes and in the open air

to sing the hmyns of the Arians, and to listen to them;
and instead of relying simply on his eloquence, although he was the most eloquent of preachers, he developed the psalmody of his own Church. Bardesanes,
the Gnostic, composed hymns and had them arranged
to popular melodies, in order to propagate Gnosticism.
Ephraem Syrus fought the heresy like a wise man, by
writing hymns himself, and encouraging the faithful to
sing them. Even Augustine wrote an elaborate hymn
to fortify his people against the Donatists. In later
times, the doctrines of the Lollards and the doctrines
of the Reformers were propagated by popular singing.
Descending later still, Charles Wesley's hymns and
the animating melodies which were the delight of
the early Methodists did as much for the triumphs of
Methodism as John Wesley's sermons. And the sacred
songs which Mr. Sankey taught us to sing were hardly
less important in promoting the recent revivals of
religious earnestness in many parts of England than
Mr. Moody's preaching.

I have heard that there are many congregations in
America where nearly the whole of the singing is left
to the choir. There is only one hymn—so I have
been told—which the people are expected to sing. It
would be impertinent in a stranger to criticise your
ecclesiastical customs, and perhaps the information
which I have received is incorrect; but if any such
custom began to show itself in England I should be dismayed. There is, indeed, no conceivable reason why
people should not worship with all their hearts while

they are listening to an anthem sung by a choir, as well as when they are listening to a prayer offered by a minister. Some of the loftier and some of the more pathetic musical expressions of religious thought and feeling are beyond the reach of ordinary congregations. They must be entrusted to cultivated voices, trained to sing together. Nor can I see why those who listen in peace to a solitary voice from the pulpit should be shocked and scandalised if sometimes they hear only a solitary voice from the choir. If the singing is for mere display we ought to recoil from it, just as we ought to recoil from preaching which is for mere display. If the singing is devout, whether it is a quartett or a solo, it may be a beautiful and noble part of Christian worship.

But the congregations that always leave the singing to the choir, and never sing at all, or that sing very rarely, or that sing languidly and without any vigour and heartiness, do not know what they miss. In nearly all great revivals of religion the common people themselves have been inspired with a passion for singing. They have sung their creed: it seemed the freest and most natural way of declaring their triumphant belief in great Christian truths —forgotten or denied in previous times of spiritual depression, and now restored to their rightful place in the thought and life of the Church. Song has expressed and intensified to enthusiasm their new faith, their new joy, their new determination to do the will of God. Song has consoled them in their sorrows, and sustained their courage in the presence of danger. When a great assembly—in a church or on the hill-side—has united in a mournful confession of sin, or a pathetic appeal to the Divine mercy, or in exultant thanksgiving for salvation, there has been created in a thousand hearts that vivid consciousness of sharing a common spiritual life which gives new energy to religious faith and new depth to religious emotion. When we find each other we are in the right way to find God. Sometimes, no doubt, when listening to a solitary singer — as when listening to a solitary speaker — a whole congregation may become conscious of sharing a common fear, a common sorrow, a common hope, a common trust, a common joy; but this consciousness of a universal sympathy is far more certainly and far more strongly developed when the common emotion gives pathos and tenderness, vehemence and energy, to the great wave of song which every voice, the rudest as well as the most cultivated, assists to swell. This, I believe, explains in part the power which psalmody exerts over the religious life; and I think that the explanation is confirmed by the fact that it is the songs which people have sung with others which they delight to sing alone. While they sing, they recover in some measure the consciousness of fellowship with other Christian souls.

Believing that popular psalmody is to be valued—not for its mere æsthetic effect, but as a means of developing and realising the communion of saints — I think that you should try to get good congregational singing. And by good congregational singing I mean singing which answers the purpose for which we wish the people to sing. The singing ought to be free from the faults which will make it intolerable to persons of cultivated musical taste, but it ought not to be of a kind in which only persons of cultivated musical taste can join. An ordinary congregation may sing in good time and with considerable expression tunes in which the rhythm is well marked, tunes which have a real melody in them, and in which the melody is not too difficult. These are the tunes with which we ought to be satisfied. To sing even these as they ought to be sung, most congregations will require some instruction. Judging, indeed, from the manner in which Mr. Sankey's songs were suddenly caught up by immense congregations in England, there are some melodies which, as soon as they are heard, people who never sang before, cannot help singing. The Pentecostal "gift of tongues" seemed to have come again in a new form; it was a "gift of song." But the wonders of Pentecost are not to be expected in ordinary times, and perhaps even the most beautiful of the melodies which Mr. Sankey has collected or composed for great revival services are not all that the Church requires for its ordinary worship. Instruction in singing will be necessary if your congregation is to sing well.

In novels, from which we Englishmen learn most of what we know about your American country life, and in some popular American biographies, I remember to have seen the "singing-school" mentioned very fre-

quently, and in a manner which suggested that the
"singing-school" is one of the most popular of American institutions; but I do not remember to have heard
of its existence in your larger cities. Perhaps this
is because the people in your cities have less time on
their hands than the people in country places, or because there are more exciting amusements accessible to
them. Whatever the reasons may be, those of you who
may become city pastors should encourage your congregations to learn to sing well enough to sing in church
on Sunday. If musical cultivation is generally diffused,
an occasional meeting of the congregation for "practice" is all that will be necessary; but if the people
know nothing of music, you should try to arrange for a
congregational singing-class. In England, when large
masses of our population did not know how to read,
the Churches said that every man, woman, and child in
a Christian country ought to be able to read the Bible,
and established schools to teach reading. If people
do not know how to sing, I think that the Churches
should say that every man, woman, and child in a
Christian congregation ought to be able to sing hymns,
and should establish classes to teach singing.

The minister should take care that the tunes which
are selected for the hymns are tunes which the people
will be able to sing, and, what is equally important,
tunes which the people will like to sing. I have heard
complaints in England that organists and leaders of
choirs are a touchy, sensitive race, impatient of ministerial interference, more anxious to display their own

powers than to assist unmusical people to sing their best; but I have never had the kind of experience which seems to have troubled some of my ministerial brethren. I cannot pretend to any scientific knowledge of music; but I have always held myself responsible for the whole service, and my responsibility has been frankly and cordially recognised by the gentlemen who have superintended the musical arrangements of the church.

Very much mischief might be averted if, in the selection of the organist and the choir-master, Churches remembered that the spirit of the man who has charge of the music is at least as important as his musical skill. If *your* only anxiety is to appoint a very fine player, the chances are that when you have appointed him *his* only anxiety will be to show how finely he can play; and if in appointing a choir-master you think of nothing except his musical taste and his skill in selecting and conducting a choir, you have no right to be surprised if he justifies your appointment by thinking of nothing but his choir and the artistic excellence of their singing.

The choice of hymns will, of course, be absolutely in your own hands. Some ministers act on the principle that a service should be a perfect unity, and their hymns are as far as possible in the same tone as their sermons. I venture to think that this principle is a false one, and that, speaking generally and leaving special occasions to be governed by a special rule, the hymns should be complementary to the sermon both in subject and in feeling. It is unwise to keep the minds and hearts of the people under a monotonous strain for an hour and a half. They become weary, and it is a relief to them when the service closes. There are great varieties of mood, of external condition, and of spiritual interest in the congregation, which we ought to try to recognise. While there should be no abrupt and violent transition from one part of the service to the part which follows it, I think there should be movement and change. When I am at home, if the sermon is hard and logical, I like to have two or three hymns throbbing with emotion; if the sermon is predominantly ethical, I look for hymns which give free play to lofty spiritual thought and desire; if the sermon is meant for light-hearted, happy people, who are in the full vigour of their strength, I generally take care that there is at least one hymn for the weary and the sorrowful. The hymn immediately before the sermon should, I think, be in harmony rather than in unison with it. Nothing can be a better preparation for a sermon on the mercy of God than a lofty hymn of worship, celebrating the glory of His holiness; and, on the other hand, a hymn on the infinite love of God is an admirable preparation for a sermon on His inflexible righteousness. Even when a hymn is sung immediately after the sermon, it is not always wise to make it a direct continuation of the sermon itself. If we have been preaching on the Divine majesty, the people will sometimes put their whole heart most easily into a hymn on the Divine pity and goodness; and after a sermon on the future triumphs of the kingdom of Christ, we shall sometimes do well to ask them to sing a hymn in which they consecrate themselves to present Christian work.

It is one of the infelicities of a minister when preaching away from home that he often finds all the hymns selected for him when he goes into the vestry on Sunday morning. But even when he is at home he is sometimes in a difficulty: the hymn-book may have very few good hymns in it. I have no intimate knowledge of the hymn-books in common use by the American Churches; but if, after giving a fair trial to the book which you find in your Church when you are elected to the pastorate, you discover that it is a bad one, you should try by gentle means to induce the people to make a change. I know a book—not an American book—in which large numbers of the hymns are so chilly, that if you put a thermometer into it, the mercury sinks many degrees below zero. Cold hymns —no matter what fire there may be in the preaching —will encourage a cold and heartless religion; and weak, sentimental hymns will encourage a weak, sentimental religion. On the other hand, hymns full of generous trust, of ardent, reverential love, of manly vigour, of thanksgiving, of hope, of joy, will train the people to a noble, masculine, and impassioned piety.

If you can get it, have a book large enough to give ample variety of choice. In a collection containing only three or four hundred hymns, ministers and Churches are "cribb'd, cabin'd, and confin'd." "But a large book is very heavy." Yes, four or five ounces heavier than a small one: and shall we impoverish the worship of the Church for the sake of having four or five ounces less to carry from home to church and back again, or for the sake of having four or five ounces less to hold in our hands when we stand up to sing? "But a large book is expensive." Well, suppose it costs forty or fifty cents more than a small one: a hymn-book will last at least ten years, and the difference of the cost will be four or five cents a year. Is the difference of sufficient importance to justify the harm inflicted on the very life of the Church by the use of a book in which you look in vain for the hymns which express some of the most vivid thoughts and some of the strongest emotions with which the Church is inspired? In England some congregations which do not hesitate to spend five or six thousand dollars in decorating their Church, grudge a thousand for a new hymn-book. I would far rather preach in a mean, dingy, ugly building, than use a poor collection of hymns. "But no congregation ever uses more than three or four hundred hymns, even if the hymn-book contains a thousand." I doubt it, unless the other six or seven hundred are not worth singing. But if it were so, we should remember that no two congregations will sing the same three or four hundred hymns, even if they use the same book. What I ask for is variety of choice.

We should have hymns enough to enable the people to express in sacred song all the moods and experiences of their changing life. It is my impression that some ministers have not discovered how wonderfully hymns may consecrate the common thoughts and common feelings of men. When they come to church on a bright spring morning, a hymn may transfigure and exalt the physical and æsthetic delight with which they welcome the returning life of Nature.

> " The glory of the Spring, how sweet !
>   The new-born life, how glad !
> 'What joy the happy earth to greet,
>   In new bright raiment clad.
>
>   *   *   *   *
>
> " Divine Renewer ! Thee I bless,
>   I greet Thy going forth ;
>   I love Thee in the loveliness
>   Of Thy renewèd earth.
>
> " But O these wonders of Thy grace,
>   These nobler works of Thine,
>   These marvels sweeter far to trace,
>   These new births more divine.
>
>   *   *   *   *
>
> " Creator Spirit, work in me
>   These wonders sweet of Thine !
>   Divine Renewer, graciously
>   Renew this heart of mine."—T. H. GILL.

And when

> " Summer suns are glowing
>   Over land and sea,
>   Happy light is flowing
>   Bountiful and free ; "

it is a good thing for the congregation to rise from the visible splendour, and to exult that

> "God's free mercy streameth
>   Over all the world,
> And His banner gleameth
>   Everywhere unfurled.
> Broad and deep and glorious
>   As the heaven above,
> Shines in might victorious
>   His eternal love."

When farmers come to church through a kindly rain that is falling after a long drought, why should we be satisfied with a sentence of thanksgiving in the prayer? Let them sing—

> "The river of God
>   The pastures hath bless'd,
> The dry wither'd sod
>   In greenness is dress'd.
>
> "And every fold
>   Shall teem with its sheep,
> With harvests of gold
>   The fields shall be deep.
>
> "The vales shall rejoice
>   With laughter and song,
> And man's grateful voice
>   The music prolong."—A. L. P.

And when in some village on the coast of Maine, or Massachusetts, or Rhode Island, a congregation is gathered on a stormy winter afternoon, and there are many hearts filled with anxiety about husbands, brothers, sons, who are likely to have a rough and perhaps a dangerous night on the Atlantic, with what a depth of feeling will they sing—

> "Eternal Father, strong to save,
>   Whose arm hath bound the restless wave,

> Who bidst the mighty ocean deep
> Its own appointed limits keep ;
> O hear us when we cry to Thee
> For those in peril on the sea."—W. WHITING.

Sometimes our hymns should take a wider range. The Jewish psalms are full of thanksgivings to God for His great goodness to the Jewish nation, for the pleasant country which He had given them, for the deliverances which He had wrought for them in hours of national peril. They recall the memory of the great men He had raised up among them — " Moses his servant, and Aaron whom he had chosen ; " Samuel the prophet, and David the king. There are lamentations over public calamities, and vehement appeals to the Divine pity. Is there any reason why the American people should not praise God for His goodness to themselves ? This vast continent, stretching from the Atlantic to the Pacific—is it not the land which God gave to your fathers ? The skies that bend over you in Connecticut and Ohio—are they not bright with the same sun that shone in the old days on the fields of Bethlehem, when David watched his father's sheep ? Is there any reason why you should not translate into new forms the ancient strain of the Psalmist—" The heavens are thine, the earth also is thine ; as for the world and the fulness thereof, thou hast created them " ? " Tabor and Hermon," sang the Psalmist, " shall rejoice in thy name,"—and have the mountains of this New World no songs of praise for Him ? Have they forgotten the God by whose strength their eternal foundations were laid ? or do they seem to be silent, only because the ears which ought to catch their music are heavy and dull?

Has God wrought no deliverances for you and for your fathers? Has He not brought you through great sufferings and great dangers? Can you not say, like the ancient saints, "We went through fire and through water, but thou broughtest us out into a wealthy place"? Has He not taught your hands to war and your fingers to fight? In times of fear and sore perplexity, has He not sent you men of noble courage and great sagacity and stainless devotion to the public good? Why should you not sing of the mercy of God which has followed this majestic Union of States all the days of its life, and confess that it is to God that you owe all your greatness and wealth and power?

The history of the Jews is our history. Our religious life still receives strength and guidance from the faith of Abraham, the troubles of Jacob, the exodus from Egypt, and the wanderings in the wilderness. I can therefore sing with all my heart about the national blessings which God bestowed upon the Jewish race three thousand years ago, whether in the rugged verse which rose from many a wild glen and many a lonely moor in Scotland when the Covenanters were hunted down by the Stuarts, verse which blended the fires of devotion with the fires of patriotism, and added the courage of saints to the courage of heroes :—

"To Him great kings who overthrew,
For He hath mercy ever;

> Yea famous kings in battle slew,
> For His grace faileth never.
> E'en Sihon, king of Amorites,
> For He hath mercy ever;
> And Og, the king of Bashanites,
> For His grace faileth never : "

or in the smoother lines of Dr. Watts :—

> " Great monarchs fell beneath His hand ;
> Victorious is His sword ;
> While Israel took the promised land,
> And faithful is His word."

But many things have happened since then—since the Jews crossed the Red Sea, and since they smote the Hittite and the Amorite, the Canaanite, the Perizzite, the Hivite, and the Jebusite. God "made known his ways unto Moses, and his acts unto the children of Israel," but "he fainteth not, neither is he weary ; " and when I am conducting the worship of Englishmen I remember that England, too, has had its history, and I am not such an atheist as to suppose that in this history God has had no part. It seems monstrous for us to sing about God's goodness to the Jews and never to sing about His goodness to ourselves ; and in these times when we are threatened with a return of dark and poisonous superstitions which we thought had passed away for ever, I am thankful for hymns in which the people can exult in the remembrance of the statesmen, the poets, the preachers, the soldiers, the saints, who, under God, accomplished in former centuries our redemption from sacerdotal tyranny. Let us thank God for sending to the Jews in the time of trouble, Gideon and Jephthah and Barak and Samson; but devout Englishmen have quite as much reason for thanking Him that He sent Wycliffe and Latimer and Cromwell and Milton, to fight and to suffer for the faith and freedom of their own country. "O that men would praise the Lord for his goodness, and for his wonderful works to the children of men." For a Christian congregation in London, Birmingham, Manchester, or Liverpool, to thank God for the defeat of Sihon, king of the Amorites, and Og, king of Bashan, and not to thank Him for the defeat of the Spanish Armada; to thank Him for the destruction of Pharaoh, and not for the destruction of the Stuarts; to thank Him for the military triumphs of David, and not for the glory of the Commonwealth and for the Revolution of 1688; would be as irrational as to thank Him for the corn that was threshed out on the threshing-floor of Araunah the Jebusite, and to refuse to thank Him for the harvest in Kent and Essex and Norfolk last autumn.

What I have just been saying rests upon a principle which has an important relation to the whole substance and method of our religious thought. Our preaching deals largely with a very wonderful history. But the story of what happened in the tents of Abraham, Isaac, and Jacob; the wars and captivities of the Jewish people, their national sins and their national chastisements; the heroism of their prophets, the crimes of their priests and their kings; would have very little to do with the lives of Americans and Englishmen in the nineteenth century, if the history were not also a revelation—a revelation of the living God, who is the same yesterday, to-day, and for ever. The teaching and the miracles of our Lord Jesus Christ Himself, His death, resurrection, and ascension into heaven, derive their supreme importance from the fact that they originated and revealed the relations which exist at this hour between God and ourselves. Our faith rests upon a history, because the history reveals the God in whom we live and move and have our being.

It is possible, however, so to treat both the Old Testament and the New as to create the impression that, although in distant lands and distant centuries God was active in the affairs of men, He is active no longer; that His intimate relations to mankind were suddenly broken off eighteen hundred years ago; that since then He has left the world to itself, with nothing more than a wonderful tradition of a diviner and more glorious age.

Such an impression is utterly destructive of religious faith. Men instinctively refuse to accept a creed which is only a tradition. The sun is shining still; the tides still ebb and flow; every spring the earth clothes itself with fresh grass and flowers; and every autumn a new harvest falls under the sickle. And the intellectual life of man is still restless, eager, and enterprising. From generation to generation it has continued to make new conquests—widening the region of human knowledge and augmenting by its discoveries the wealth and power of the race. In the moral and social and political life of nations there is also constant movement and change. Ancient wisdom offers no solution of the problems which task the strength of every new age. Laws once salutary and just become obsolete. Venerable institutions by which great races have been disciplined to greatness gradually decay. In every country where there is any moral vigour, where society is not utterly corrupt, where political government is not a rigid despotism, there is an incessant struggle for reform.

Shall we look on all this activity with suspicion and alarm? Why should we? We, of all men,—we whose very function it is to assert the glory of God, should be the most eager to acknowledge the splendours of human genius, and to celebrate the intellectual triumphs of the race; for "the inspiration of the Almighty giveth them understanding." We, of all men —we who have consecrated our strength to the study of the life and the thought of the Lord Jesus Christ, should be the first to honour the men who with equal patience and enthusiasm are investigating the structure and laws of the material universe, and to us their work should have an exceptional sacredness. They are enlarging our knowledge of Christ Himself; " for by him were all things created, that are in heaven, and that are in earth, visible and invisible, whether they be thrones, or dominions, or principalities, or powers: all things were created by him and for him." And we, of all men, we who are constantly insisting that neither individuals nor nations can prosper unless they learn the Divine will and do it, should watch with the keenest sympathy and should warmly encourage the efforts of reformers and statesmen to discover and apply the laws on which national prosperity depends.

If, indeed, in the presence of this exciting and perpetual activity—this constant extension of man's knowledge of the Universe; this prolonged and generous and not unsuccessful struggle to lessen the evils of man's condition, and to secure the triumph of righteousness and truth—we had to confess that in the sphere of Divine revelation with which we have to deal there has been no movement for eighteen centuries, that through the whole of this vast and desolate period God has shown no living interest in the fortunes of mankind, we might well have reason to fear that the world would refuse to listen to us.

But we have no such confession to make. God's relations to the human race are still real and intimate. His activity in human affairs has never been interrupted. The revelation of Himself in human history is still incomplete. He has not left us, in these last ages, with no other sources of knowledge of Him than those which are contained in His material works, or in the irreversible laws which are constantly receiving fresh illustrations from the social and political vicissitudes of nations. Nor has He even left us to make what we can of that supernatural revelation which culminated in the life and death of our Lord Jesus Christ.

"He fainteth not, neither is he weary." I see the proofs of His mercy and power in the triumphs of the gospel on the day of Pentecost; but other triumphs of the gospel achieved in later centuries manifest the same mercy and the same power. The conversion of St. Paul was an illustration of the Divine grace; but every successful preacher is continually witnessing illustrations of the same grace in the conversion of men by his own ministry. Divine acts are not less Divine because they do not happen to be recorded in the canonical Scriptures. The last report of your Board of Foreign Missions is the continuation by an inferior hand of the story which was begun in the Acts of the Apostles.

The miracles of earlier ages have ceased; they are no longer necessary; they ought to have taught us to recognise the permanent manifestation of the power of God in the orderly movements of the material universe. We no longer possess the special illumination which was granted to the sacred writers, enabling them to bear authoritative testimony to the presence of God in events for which historical philosophy might have attempted to offer a natural explanation; but we ought to have learnt from the Holy Scriptures that the common lives of men and the common history of nations are under the Divine control.

Gentlemen, I trust that you will not be mere religious antiquarians. You will assert the present authority, you will preach the present love, of the living God. It will be your endeavour to make men understand that the dream which came to Jacob at Bethel is a dream no longer; that in Christ, heaven and earth, God and man, have been brought together. You will teach men that only in God's light can they see light, and that if they devoutly seek for it the light of God will come to them, and will illuminate both the ancient Scriptures and our modern life. You will insist that the moral and spiritual perfection to which we are called is beyond our reach until we receive the power of God; and you will warn them against the superstition of supposing that they can derive moral and spiritual strength either from Divine promises written in a book, or from the memory of the manifestations of Divine glory and goodness in remote ages. The promises are intended to command our faith in God's present help: the history of His great and merciful deeds in former times illustrates the love and the power to which we can appeal in our own days. It will be the object of your ministry to prevail upon your congregations to recognise the authority of God, and to honour Him, in all the common affairs of life as well as in their religious worship and in what they call their religious work; in their homes, their trades, their professions, their amusements; in literature, politics, and art. To accomplish this object you must believe—and you must make them believe—that God is still "a God nigh at hand, and not afar off."

Respect the rights of the past: assert the rights of the present. Sing the songs in which the saints of past generations expressed their trust and joy in God, but do not refuse the songs of devout men of our own days. Be grateful for the pathos and solemnity of Gregorian chants; be grateful, too, for the brighter and more triumphant strains which have been written in later times by men who have consecrated their genius to the service of the Church. Welcome all truth—the truth in that glorious " Psalm of Creation " which appears on the first page of the Jewish Scriptures, and which reveals the personal relations of God to the universe; the truth in the latest demonstrated results of scientific inquiry which reveal the methods by which through unmeasured ages God has been bringing the order of this fair world out of darkness and chaos. To you, America must be sacred as well as Judæa; and you will teach men that in New York and Washington, in Chicago and Charleston and San Francisco, they may be as near to God as were the priests on the day when the temple was consecrated, and when they " could not enter the house of the Lord " because it was filled with His glory.

After what I have said in previous lectures you will not suspect me of depreciating that knowledge of the truths of the Christian faith which we acquire by the study of Exegetical and Dogmatic Theology. But this knowledge, invaluable as it is, will prove inadequate to the exigencies of your ministry. Is there not a direct vision—what has been called an intuition—of the great objects of faith? It is true that the revelation which was made to us by the Lord Jesus Christ

Himself, and which was illustrated by His apostles, must constitute the very substance of all Christian thought. No man who has discovered the dignity and glory of Christ, and who understands the greatness of the commission which He gave to the apostles, will ever speak as though it were possible for us to become independent either of Him or them. But the New Testament itself may be read in the natural light of the human intellect or in the light of the Spirit of God ; and until we read it in the diviner illumination we have no such knowledge of it as we need.

There are very many men whose personal history is a commentary on my meaning. Their creed in its logical expression is very much the same to-day that it was twenty years ago, but they would tell you that though the same it is wonderfully different. The Divinity of our Lord Jesus Christ, for instance, they had long ceased to doubt. They had examined the controversy, and their minds were made up. They believed that He was God manifest in the flesh. Yes —they believed this, just as *we* believe that some great painting we see in a picture gallery is the work of Murillo or Da Vinci. The catalogue tells us so, and perhaps gives the history of the painting from the time it left the easel till it was hung on those very walls. But an artist comes in, and he does not require to look at the catalogue to learn that it was an illustrious master who created those gracious outlines and that rich depth of colour. He knows that the work could not have come from any common hand ; he *sees* the genius in which you and I, perhaps, only *believe*. Time was when he, too, wanted the catalogue with its documentary proofs; he may even now be obliged to appeal to those proofs against any who doubt, for his own perceptions cannot be made theirs; but for himself evidence of that kind has become unnecessary: he knows the hand of the master on the canvas as we know the hand of a friend in a letter. And so there are many who would tell you that their *belief* in the Divinity of our Lord Jesus Christ, which once rested, and rested immovably, on granite foundations of authority, has passed into something higher and better: they read the Gospels and they see God in the face of Jesus Christ. It is as though they had been with Him on the Mount of Transfiguration, and had beheld His glory. Nay, there is something better than that; for the splendour which was seen by Peter, James, and John, soon faded away; it became a mere remembrance; while the glory which they behold in Christ is like that which shone in the Holy of Holies, a permanent witness to the presence of God.

But in the creed of many of us are there not doctrines, facts, which have never yet risen out of the region of intellectual belief into that of immediate spiritual vision? Some of us can remember the kind of transformation which passed upon "the principles of the doctrine of Christ" at the time of our conversion: must we not acknowledge that there are other truths which have not even yet been thus transformed? What I wish to say is that every one of you, before your life in this university is over, should endeavour to secure from God the immediate and supernatural revelation of those great truths which must constitute the strength of your ministry. It is unnecessary that I should tell you how you are to secure it. Solitary meditation ; earnest prayer for Divine light ; devout, quiet, yet persistent efforts to see things as they are ; fellowship with Christian men, who, though they may have less learning than yourselves, have lived longer than you have lived in the presence of God ; a loyal discharge of all common duties, practical fidelity to the light which God has already given you — these will be rewarded by a gradual, sometimes by a sudden, manifestation of vast provinces of the spiritual universe. Do not ask for the solution of the difficulties by which theologians have been perplexed and divided ; try to know at first-hand—to see for yourselves—the facts about which the Church is agreed. Human sin —endeavour to see it as God Himself sees it. Entreat God so to reveal to you His love for the human race, that it may become as real and vivid to you as the love which will change your mother's voice into music when you go home again, and will fill her face with light. Knowledge of this kind will give depth to your religious life, security and stability to your faith, and power to your ministry.

Perhaps some of you will reply that the truths of which I have been speaking are the mere commonplaces of the Christian Faith, and that if a preacher is to have any real force he must be original. Well, if

I may suggest another and very inferior reason for seeking the kind of knowledge I have been describing, I will add that it will invest your preaching with the charm of originality. I remember that to many of the students of my own day originality appeared to be one of the chief excellences of a sermon. Perhaps to some of you it may have the same supreme attractiveness. Eloquence, you are perhaps disposed to speak of very lightly, as though it were a mere trick by which some men are able to invest with a meretricious brilliance the poorest and dreariest platitudes. That practical knowledge of the human heart and of human life which constitutes the power of some successful preachers, you have, in all probability, not yet learned to appreciate at its true value, and you cannot understand how it is that the men who have nothing else, achieve such considerable results. I am speaking, you must remember, as if you had the same way of thinking about preachers that prevailed at my own college when I was a student. We thought that there were hardly any sermons to be heard that were worth listening to. Popular ministers were the favourite objects—well, not of our contempt—but of our kindly and condescending patronage, except that now and then we felt righteously indignant that they should have won their reputation so cheaply. But originality was the pearl of great price: we were ready to sell all that we had to buy it.

Our estimate of the supreme worth of originality was not altogether false ; only, I think, that we sometimes failed to recognise it where it existed, and were sometimes imposed upon by a miserably paltry imitation of it. We have gradually found the cheats out. We have discovered that very much that seemed fresh and wonderful was only a grotesque distortion of the most familiar truths, or a weak and servile imitation of the mere intellectual mannerism of some writer of great—or, perhaps, even of second or third rate—genius. Originality of that kind is within the reach of every man that is fool enough to care for it. It is no pearl of great price, which all your wealth will hardly purchase; it is what men slanderously call mere "Brummagem jewellery," to be bought for a few poor coppers.

True originality is something different from this. It is not to be acquired by the methods which some men adopt to obtain it. You may become singular, odd, ridiculous, absurd, by trying not to think and speak like other people, but original — never.[1] If you want to be an original preacher, look at heaven and hell, life and death, sin and holiness, with your own eyes; listen for yourselves to the voice of God; ask Him to reveal to you the glory of His love, the steadfastness of His truth, the energy of His righteousness, and tell the world what you have heard and seen. Pierce to the heart of things. Get at the facts which lie behind appearances. In this way originality will come to you when you are not seeking

[1] "Quand on court après l'esprit, on attrape la sottise." Montesquieu: "Pensées Diverses."

it. It will be unconscious,[1] and therefore will not minister to your conceit; it will be part of your very life, and will therefore characterise more or less all your sermons, and not merely those on which you have been able to spend most time and labour; it will not wear out after the first years of your ministry are over, but will remain with you as long as you have the clear vision of God, and as long as the spiritual universe lies open to you. While it will command for you the respect of those who are capable of forming a true judgment of your power, it will not provoke the silly wonder of conceited and undisciplined minds. It will save you from the humiliation of their foolish idolatry; it will be out of the reach of their critical admiration; but it will enable you to accomplish for them and for all your people the great objects of your ministry.

Among the truths which with special earnestness you should ask God to reveal to you by the light of His Spirit, so that you may have a direct and original knowledge of it, is the truth of Christ's presence with you in your work. His own words, "Lo, I am with you always"—words which express a fact rather than a promise—are directly connected with the command to disciple all nations. If this presence is revealed to you all your ministerial work will be transfigured. The weight of anxiety which, if you are

---

[1] "Voici comme je définis le talent : un don que Dieu nous a fait en secret, et que nous révélons sans le savoir." Montesquieu: "Pensées Diverses."

alone, will almost crush you; the consciousness of weakness which, if you do not see that Christ is near, will sometimes force from you a bitter and despairing cry for release from the responsibilities of the ministry, will vanish. Saturday night comes, and you are thinking of the services of Sunday: your heart will leap when you say to yourself, "Christ will meet the congregation with me." You may be troubled by the fear that the fervour of your earnestness for the salvation of men has cooled; but while seeking to rekindle it your trouble will be lessened, for you will say, "Christ will be with me, and Christ's earnestness will be intense as ever." You have done your best in the way of preparation; but perhaps you have been interrupted in your work, or your brain has been sluggish, and you know that in what you have prepared there is less than the usual force and fire, but you will not be despondent; you will say, "I have done what I could; Christ will be with me, and He can invest this poor discourse of mine with power." Your own sense of Christ's presence may not be so vivid as it has been, but you will say, "Still He will be with me, and He will bless the people beyond my hopes, and theirs."

It would be of no avail for us to preach at all if He were not with us; we shall preach to little purpose if we do not believe that He is with us. It is still true that "he that soweth the good seed is the Son of man:" only as we are filled with His life and His thought shall we preach anything that will deserve to be called a gospel. If *we* always have the consciousness of Christ's presence our congregations will discover it, and the discovery will assist to strengthen their faith in Him.

It may be that there are laws which determine the manifestations of the supernatural power of Christ; it is clear that these manifestations are related to the truth which is preached, to the spirit and manner in which we preach it, and to the earnestness and faith with which we entreat Him to have mercy on mankind. We have to discover and to satisfy the conditions on which the success of our preaching depends. But, after all, the quickening of the souls of men, and their sanctification, are as truly the personal acts of Christ as were any of the miracles of His earthly history. It is He who must forgive the sins of which we speak to our people; it is He who must renew their hearts; it is He who must give them strength for right-doing. It is not truth merely—no matter how sacred; it is not spiritual motive merely—no matter how urgent, how pathetic, how glorious, how appalling; it is not our own earnestness—no matter how deep and how impassioned; that will move men to penitence, draw them to God, enable them to keep the Divine law. We have to rely ultimately on the power of the Spirit, and the power of the Spirit is the revelation of the presence of Christ. The presence of Christ is assured to us by His own words. To disregard it, to think only of how we ourselves can stir the hearts of our hearers and instruct their understandings, is to be guilty of an atheistic presumption which will utterly destroy the effectiveness of our ministry.

Gentlemen, yours is a noble vocation. To be the ally of Christ in His great endeavour to save the world, — with Him to assert the authority of the throne and law of God; with Him to support human weakness in its vacillating endeavours to do the Divine will; to inspire the sinful with trust in the Divine mercy; to console sorrow; to awaken in the hearts of the poor, the weak, and the desolate, the consciousness of their relations to the Infinite and Eternal God; to exalt and dignify the lives of old men and maidens, young men and children, by revealing to them the things unseen and eternal which surround them now, and the mysterious, awful, glorious life which lies beyond death—this is a great work. There is nothing on earth comparable to it. Whatever genius you have, whatever learning, whatever native moral force, whatever energy of spiritual inspiration, will all find their freest and loftiest service in the work to which you are consecrated. And in the ministry, even the humblest faculties, if used with devout earnestness, may, through alliance with the power of God, achieve great results.

However obscure your ministerial position may be, to whatever discomforts you may have to submit, however bitter may be your disappointments, I trust that your work will be always invested with the dignity and glory which now invest it, when in your noblest and most sacred hours you anticipate in imagination the years which are stretching before you. Give Christ your best. Be faithful to Him—be faithful to your people—be faithful to yourselves—and you will not have to exclaim when your life is over, "All is vanity and vexation of spirit." You will thank God that He appointed you in this world to a service which was the most perfect preparation for the larger life, the loftier activities, the everlasting glory of the world to come.

www.ingramcontent.com/pod-product-compliance
Lightning Source LLC
Chambersburg PA
CBHW022026240426
43667CB00042B/1206